Tea: The Drink That Changed the World

LCM 2003

Tea

The Drink That Changed the World

by Laura C. Martin

TUTTLE PUBLISHING
Tokyo • Rutland, Vermont • Singapore

Published by Tuttle Publishing, an imprint of Periplus Editions (HK) Ltd., with editorial offices at 364 Innovation Drive, North Clarendon, Vermont 05759 U.S.A.

Many of the decorative illustrations in this book are from the classic *All About Tea* by William H. Ukers, which was published in 1935 by the Tea and Coffee Trade Journal Company. www.teaandcoffee.net

LIBRARY OF CONGRESS CATALOGING-IN-PUBLICATION DATA
Martin, Laura C.
Tea : the drink that changed the world / Laura C. Martin.
    p. cm.
Includes bibliographical references.
ISBN-13: 978-0-8048-3724-8 (hardcover)
ISBN-10: 0-8048-3724-4 (hardcover)
1. Tea—History. 2. Tea—Social aspects. I. Title.
GT2905.M36 2007
394.1'2—dc22

                          2006037833

ISBN-13: 978-0-8048-3724-8
ISBN-10: 0-8048-3724-4

DISTRIBUTED BY
North America, Latin America & Europe
Tuttle Publishing, 364 Innovation Drive, North Clarendon, VT 05759-9436 U.S.A.
Tel: 1 (802) 773-8930 Fax: 1 (802) 773-6993 info@tuttlepublishing.com www.tuttlepublishing.com

Japan
Tuttle Publishing, Yaekari Building, 3rd Floor, 5-4-12 Osaki, Shinagawa-ku, Tokyo 141 0032
Tel: (81) 3 5437-0171 Fax: (81) 3 5437-0755 tuttle-sales@gol.com

Asia Pacific
Berkeley Books Pte. Ltd., 130 Joo Seng Road #06-01, Singapore 368357
Tel: (65) 6280-1330 Fax: (65) 6280-6290 inquiries@periplus.com.sg www.periplus.com

Indonesia
PT Java Books Indonesia, Kawasan Industri Pulogadung, JI. Rawa Gelam IV No. 9, Jakarta 13930
Tel: (62) 21 4682-1088 Fax: (62) 21 461-0207 cs@javabooks.co.id

First edition
11 10 09 08 07   10 9 8 7 6 5 4 3 2 1

Printed in the United States of America

TUTTLE PUBLISHING® is a registered trademark of Tuttle Publishing, a division of Periplus Editions (HK) Ltd.

This book is dedicated in loving memory to my parents,
Ken Coogle, 1907–2005, and Lois Coogle, 1915–2006,
who both had an insatiable thirst for knowledge.

CONTENTS

INTRODUCTION

I love tea and drink a lot of it. Part of my attraction lies in the simple act of making the tea, of stopping my daily routine to boil water and watch the tea steep until the clear water turns any number of colors, from pale gold to amber to deep brown, depending on the type of tea I'm preparing. And then there is the pleasure of the first sip! Tea is more delicate than coffee, infinitely more interesting than water, healthier and more subtle than soda. It is the perfect beverage—one that can be drunk frequently and in great quantities with pleasure and without guilt. Tea, in all its complexities, offers a simultaneous feeling of calm and alertness, of health and pleasure. It is no wonder these leaves, discovered in China so long ago, have changed the world.

There is a tea produced in almost every region of the globe, and one to suit every part of the day and every mood. I begin the morning with a brisk black tea such as Keemun or perhaps a stout Irish breakfast blend. When I'm feeling adventurous, I'll try a Pu-erh from China. Throughout the day, I sip on the Japanese green tea sencha, but sometimes vary it with a green tea mixed with an herb such as hibiscus. For a special occasion, I'll "uncork" something such as the Japanese gyokuro, "Precious Dew." By late afternoon I'm ready for the clean, bright taste of a white tea, such as "Silver Needles."

I'm not alone in my love of tea. The Turkish, ranked as the highest per capita consumers of tea in the world (based on 2004 statistics), drink an average of 2.5 kilograms (5.51 pounds)—more than a thousand cups—a year per person! Turkey is followed by the United Kingdom, with 2.2 kilograms (4.85 pounds) annually, and Morocco at 1.4 kilograms (3.09 pounds). We in the United States are not even in the running, though I know I must personally help drive up the averages!

People around the world are serious about their tea, as well they should be, for tea is big business with a rich and diverse past. Since ancient times in China, when raw tea leaves were brewed to make a harsh, bitter concoction used for medicine, tea has played an important part in human lives—even though it would be centuries before processing methods were discovered that changed the taste of tea from bitter to delicious.

For many centuries, only the Chinese knew of the wonders of tea, but eventually the habit of drinking tea spread throughout Asia, and then throughout the world. Tea traveled with traders, who found it to be a popular commodity; with travelers, who appreciated the comfort of a daily cup of tea during a long journey; and, particularly in its early history, with scholars and monks. Because drinking tea soothed the mind but kept one alert and awake, Buddhist monks frequently used it as a tool for meditation. As monks traveled from one country to the next, teaching about Buddhism and meditation, they took tea with them, and so the habit of drinking tea flowed from China throughout Southeast Asia and beyond.

Monks first introduced tea to Japan in the sixth century, but it wasn't until the eighth century that cultivation began and tea became an important part of Japanese life. During the fifteenth century, tea masters in Japan developed rituals and symbolism around serving tea that resulted in the Japanese tea ceremony, which is still practiced today with such grace.

The first European port city to experience tea was Amsterdam, during the first few years of the seventeenth century. At first tea was treated as nothing more than a novelty—though a very expensive one. Tea didn't make it to London for another half-century, but once the Brits found a taste for tea, they were never the same again. The British developed such a mania for tea (fueled by the British East India Company merchants who made vast fortunes selling tea) that it quickly became part of the national culture. Tea the drink and tea the social occasion became a part of British life, for everyone from lords and ladies to the men and women of the working class.

The obsession for tea in England during the nineteenth century had devastating effects half a world away in China and India. As England expanded her imperialistic powers, she became more greedy for tea and the profits it engendered. When the British realized that trading opium for tea was more lucrative than buying tea with silver, they quickly developed a huge opium industry in India. The ruling British class in India forced local farmers to grow opium poppies in their fields, rather than food crops. The result was hunger and deprivation in India and the Opium Wars and their tragic toll in China.

Much of tea's history illustrates the never ending human story of class division—of greed, power, and wealth on one side and of hunger and poverty on the other. This was true in eighth-century China when the emperor forced peasants to produce tea instead of planting their own rice crops for food; it is equally true today in India, as many of the tea plantations are closed. The owners move on, while the workers are left on abandoned plantations with no medicine, running water, or food.

Not all of tea's history is dark and depressing, however, for it has provided, and still does provide, livelihoods for millions of people. Today many small growers throughout the world—from Southeast Asia to South America—plant and cultivate this ancient crop. And people all over the world enjoy the incomparable taste of tea.

The story of tea is the story of humankind in a nutshell, or perhaps a teacup. It includes the best and the worst of who we are and what we do. Throughout its long history, tea has been used as medicine, as an aid to meditation, as currency, as bribes, and as a means of controlling rebellions. It has been the instigation for wars and global conflicts. It has also been the reason for parties, for family gatherings, and for high-society occasions. In short, tea has touched and changed our lives as no other beverage has, connecting us all—from the workers to the monks, from the pluckers to the emperors, from the British to the Chinese, to me.

As I sit and sip yet another cup of tea, it is my hope that the story of tea will teach us lessons of humankind and of human kindness, that we will find that tea did not merely change the world, but changed humanity.

CHAPTER 1

From Shrub to Cup: An Overview

"O tea! O leaves torn from the sacred bough! O stalk,
gift born of the great gods! What joyful region bore thee?"
—*Pierre Daniel Huet (1630–1721), French scholar*

THE MAGIC OF TEA is well camouflaged, for the leaves that produce one of the tastiest of all beverages look no more exciting than the leaves of many other types of trees or shrubs. But, if picked at the right moment, processed in the correct manner, packaged and protected against humidity, mold, and other impurities, then properly brewed, these leaves produce a beverage unlike any other.

Tea has a long history as a beverage and is grown in many different places in the world. It is not surprising, therefore, that a confusing mass of terminology is used to describe the plant itself and the methods by which it has been processed during the past two thousand years. The following sections of this chapter will introduce and clarify many of these terms, as we begin to explore the complex and exciting world of tea.

NATURAL HISTORY

Some teas, such as Darjeeling, are named for the region in which they are grown and processed. Other teas have specific names but are generally only grown and processed in a particular region—Keemun from China, for example. But all true tea comes from a single species of plant, *Camellia sinensis*, which is in the family Theaceae. This family also includes other shrubs of horticultural value, such as the ornamental *Franklinia* and *Stewartia*. Although the botanical name for tea is officially *Camellia sinensis*, the tea plant is still sometimes found under many other outdated names, including *Thea viridis*, *Thea sinensis*, *Thea bohea*, *Camellia theifera*, *Camellia thea*, and *Camellia bohea*.

Camellia sinensis is an evergreen shrub that produces small aromatic flowers with white petals and numerous golden stamens. Botanists have divided this single species (*sinensis*) into two distinct varieties, *sinensis* and *assamica*. *Camellia sinensis* var. *sinensis* is indigenous to western Yunnan in China and was known for centuries (or perhaps millennia) before the assam variety was discovered. *Camellia sinensis* var. *assamica* is indigenous to the Assam region of India, and to Burma, Thailand, Laos, Cambodia, Vietnam, and southern China. Although there are many specimens of large tea plants found in the forests of these regions, tea has been cultivated for so many centuries there, and the plant crossbreeds so readily, that it is impossible to tell if these are relics of ancient plantings or truly wild, indigenous species.

Although anatomically dissimilar enough for botanists to designate them as different varieties, the two plants put forth leaves that, when processed in the same way, taste surprisingly similar. The differences in the tastes of green,

Tea plants grown to giant proportions: "The Himalaya from Rangagurrah Muttack in The Jungle of Upper Assam." After a sketch made on the spot by William Griffith, 1847

black, and oolong teas are a result of the different ways in which the leaves are processed. *Sinensis* and *assamica* cross-pollinate easily, which has resulted in any number of hybrids with varying degrees of the qualities of one or the other variety, creating a continuous range of characteristics between them.

A tea plant can be called either a tree or shrub, depending on circumstances. Left on its own under favorable conditions, a tea plant will grow to be tree-sized. In cultivation, tea plants are kept pruned to shrub size. Regular pruning cycles, which vary from every two to every four years, keep tea shrubs at about one meter (a little over three feet), a height convenient for picking the leaves.

Although the first cultivated tea plants were grown from seed, the preferred propagation method today is to take cuttings from vigorous shrubs. The cuttings are placed in nursery beds and are carefully tended for twelve to fifteen months before they are planted in the tea garden. When an individual plant reaches a height of approximately half a meter (fifteen to eighteen inches), it is cut back to within a few inches of the ground. This severe pruning causes the plant to grow in a V shape, creating a "plucking table"—a flat shape that greatly increases the number of terminal buds growing along the upper surface of the plant. Depending on the region in which they are grown, shrubs are spaced from one to one and a half meters (about three to five feet) apart.

In its native habitat, tea grew in open woodland or in the dappled shade at the borders between woodland and open field, an area that includes both sun and shade. Tea growers at lower elevations (such as Assam and Kenya) mimic this environment as closely as possible, and large trees are grown in the tea plantations for the purpose of providing shade for the tea shrubs. The most commonly used shade trees include albizzia, erythrina, gliricidia and silver oak. Shade trees not only provide needed relief from the intense light and heat, but also serve to improve soil conditions and prevent rampant growth of weeds.

In warm climates (at lower elevations), plants are ready for harvest at about two and a half years. At higher elevations, where growth is slower, it takes five years before the first leaves from a plant are ready to harvest. Tea plants

How to Grow Your Own Tea

It is certainly possible to grow a tea plant in many regions of the world. In the United States, it is hardy in horticultural growing zones 6b–9.

In cultivation, *Camellia sinensis* prefers the same growing conditions that azaleas and rhododendrons do. Provide your tea plants with sandy to loamy, well-drained soils that are either neutral or acidic. Tea plants grow best when provided with high shade, but be careful not to place them where the roots will have to compete with those of other trees. Irrigate generously, but be certain that drainage is good, to prevent the roots from rotting.

Tea plants are available from some mail-order sources. If you have access to an established plant, you can propagate a new plant via a cutting. To root a cutting (the method of propagation used by commercial growers), take a hardwood cutting from winter to late spring, dip the end in a rooting hormone (available at a garden center or nursery), and plant it in a pot with a sterile potting medium. Keep it in the pot for twelve to eighteen months before planting in the ground.

grown at lower elevations produce a greater quantity of leaves in a single growing season, but those grown at higher elevations—such as in the Darjeeling district of India where plants are grown on the lower slopes of the Himalayas—produce much finer teas.

In most regions, the best-quality tea is still picked by hand, although mechanical harvesters are becoming more and more common. Workers who harvest the leaves by hand are traditionally called pluckers. An experienced plucker can pick between thirty and thirty-five kilograms (sixty-six to seventy-seven pounds) of tea every day. For the highest-quality tea, only the first two leaves and the bud, and sometimes only the bud, are picked at any one time, and are tossed into a basket carried on the worker's back. Although leaves from each shrub may be harvested from three to five times during a single year, the quality of the leaves differs according to the season in which they were picked. "First flush," meaning the first leaves harvested in the season, are usually the best quality. "Flush" refers to a period of active growth during which the leaves can be gathered. In the Darjeeling region, the first flush lasts from March through April, the second begins in May and lasts through June, and the third occurs in autumn, from September through November. During the months between June and September, monsoon rains prevent harvesting in this region.

Depending on the variety (*assamica* or *sinensis*) and where it grows, a tea shrub can produce for at least fifty years. The greatest productivity of *Camellia sinensis* var. *sinensis* occurs during the first fifty years, although the plant will continue to produce for up to one hundred years.

TEA HARVEST AND PROCESSING

The processing methods for tea vary, according to the kind of tea desired—white, green, oolong, or black. Every tea master, just like every wine master, has a unique of way of creating a special product, but in general, the same basic steps are performed to make leaves into tea. Not every step is necessary for making each type of tea, however. Black tea, for example, involves every stage, while white tea involves only a few.

Once the buds and leaves are plucked, they are brought in from the field within two to three hours for the finest-quality tea. If the picked leaves are bruised, left unattended for too long, or allowed to get too warm, the cell walls in the leaf break down and oxidation begins, resulting in an unpleasant, bitter flavor. This must have been what the earliest tea drinkers experienced, as they plucked leaves and put them directly into boiling water, immediately starting the oxidation process. Letters and diaries from ancient China refer to tea as a bitter brew, and praise its health benefits rather than its taste. As with many other beverages, including coffee and wine, the taste of tea has been greatly enhanced by the evolution of processing methods.

The freshly plucked leaves may undergo one or more of the following processes, which are parts of what's called an orthodox method of tea processing:

1. *Withering.* Fresh, green leaves and buds are softened by withering. The leaves are placed on racks in a large, heated room, or sometimes simply allowed to air-dry in the sunshine. The purpose of withering is twofold: First, a biochemical reaction occurs, as the starch in the leaf begins to

Withering tray (after drawings by C. A. Bruce, 1838, and J. C. Houssaye, 1843)

convert to sugar. The second change is physical, as the moisture content of the leaves drops by 50 to 80 percent. The result is a soft, pliable leaf that can be rolled without breaking. Withering can take anywhere from ten to twenty-four hours, or, when white tea is processed, only about four or five hours.

Without withering, tea leaves produce an unpleasant, bitter taste. For hundreds of years, workers tested the progress of the withering process by simply squeezing a handful of leaves to see how stiff or limp they felt. Today, more accurate measurements are available in the form of NIR (near infrared) machines that measure the moisture content instantaneously, taking ten readings per second.

The desired moisture content varies from one growing region to another and depends on the characteristics of the leaves growing in a particular area. For example, tea masters of the Assam region of India prefer a soft withering, with a moisture content between 65 and 75 percent. In Sri Lanka, tea masters prefer a hard wither (a drier leaf), between 50 and 60 percent moisture.

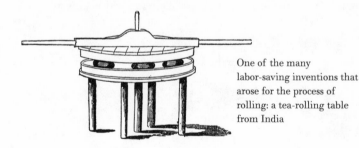

One of the many labor-saving inventions that arose for the process of rolling: a tea-rolling table from India

Rolling by hand (after drawings by C. A. Bruce, 1838, and J. C. Houssaye, 1843)

2. *Rolling.* After withering, the leaves are rolled, either by machine or (increasingly rare) by hand. This serves to twist the leaves and crush them, releasing the sap and exposing it to oxygen, which stimulates fermentation.

In some tea-processing plants, the rolled leaves are then sifted through various grades of screening to sort them by size. The larger leaf particles may be rolled a second or third time to twist and break them sufficiently for the next stage. Rolling takes approximately two hours.

3. *Oxidation.* This is the most important part of the processing procedure because it is during this stage that the flavor and value of the tea are determined. The oxidation (fermentation) stage also plays the greatest role in creating different categories of tea. For example, black tea is fully oxidized, while green and white teas are not oxidized at all.

The rolled leaves are placed on trays and spread to a thickness of three to six centimeters (one to two inches), then left in a cool, damp place to oxidize for one to three hours. Chemical reactions within the leaf cause it to heat. It is crucial to stop oxidation at the height of this reaction to obtain the best flavor from the leaves. If the temperatures get too high, the leaves taste burned; if too low, the fermentation process stops, resulting in a metallic aftertaste. During oxidation, the color of the leaves changes from green to copper, and the ultimate aroma, flavor, and color of the tea are determined.

4. *Drying, or desiccation.* The oxidized leaves are dried with hot air in a large drier and on a conveyer belt, at temperatures between 85 and 88 degrees Celsius (185 to 190.4 degrees Fahrenheit). This serves to quickly stop the fermentation process, and the copper-colored leaves turn the characteristic dark brown or black. Drying time, too, is critical because if the leaves retain too much moisture (more than 12 percent), they are subject to mold. If they are allowed to dry out too much (less than 2–3 percent humidity), they produce tea that tastes burned or flavorless.

5. *Grading, or sorting.* The dried tea leaves are separated into different leaf grades, depending on the size of the leaf particles. The different categories include whole leaf, broken leaf, fannings, and dust. In general, whole leaf (which includes the tender tips and buds) produces the finest-quality tea, while fannings and dust are generally used to make the quick-brewing teas most often used in tea bags.

Some combination of these processes is used to make each of the four main types of tea. Within each type of tea, there

"Drinking a daily cup of tea will surely starve the apothecary."

—*Chinese proverb*

are countless named varieties and brands. Blends are made by combining different varieties of the same type of tea. For example, a "breakfast blend" combines several different kinds of black tea. The processing stages for the four main varieties are:

Black tea. The leaves undergo all five processing stages and are completely oxidized.

Oolong tea. The leaves are withered and rolled, then partially oxidized (anywhere from 10 to 80 percent, but usually around 60 percent), heated, and sorted.

Green tea. Buds and leaves are withered, then rolled. The smaller and more tightly rolled, the more robust the flavor found in the tea. (For example, the type of green tea called gunpowder is composed of tiny pellets of tightly rolled leaves, and is quite robust.) After rolling, the leaves are

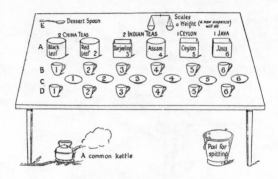

"A Suggested Retailer's Outfit for Tasting Teas." Showing a "simple but practical lesson by Mr. C. L. T. Beeching." From W. H. Ukers' *All About Tea*, the 1935 tea industry classic

immediately heated to prevent oxidation. In China, the leaves are heated by either roasting or pan-frying. In Japan, the leaves are generally steamed. Both processes result in green tea, but the flavors are different. (Consider the difference in taste between a steamed onion and a roasted one.) Japanese green tea tastes herbaceous or vegetal. China green tea has a more citrus or smoky flavor.

Matcha is a green tea that has been ground to a powder, as it was in the fifteenth century. It is still used in the Japanese tea ceremony.

White tea. This is the least processed of all teas. The Tea Council of the USA is spearheading efforts to develop an international standard definition for white tea. They have suggested the following: Tea made from either the first flush bud or the bud and one leaf, either air-dried or directly warm fired. (When "warm fired" the leaves are heated by mechanical means.) Leaves that make white tea undergo no withering, fermentation, or rolling and produce a liquid that is either pale yellow or clear. The best-known white teas are Silver Needles and White Peony, although others are quickly gaining recognition.

CTC tea, called an unorthodox tea, takes its name from the mechanical "crush, tear, and curl" process used to get cheap, uniform, but inferior tea. Tea derived from this process is generally used for blends or tea bags, and it brews quickly, in two to three minutes. CTC is often viewed as the best tea for making chai. The CTC market is very strong; some estimates state that more than 80 percent of India's tea production is CTC.

GRADES OF TEA

The four grades of black tea (whole leaf, broken leaf, fannings, and dust) vary in quality. The latter two are considered inferior and are used to bulk up more expensive teas, or to make tea bags or instant powdered teas.

Not all tea products display the grade of tea, but when they do, the following will help you determine the quality of tea you are purchasing.

 "Women are like teabags; we don't know our true strengths until we are in hot water."
    —*Eleanor Roosevelt* (*1884–1962*)

Whole Leaf

OP, or orange pekoe (pronounced peck-oh), is the most basic, or first grade, of whole-leaf black tea. The word "pekoe" comes from the Chinese word *pak-ho*, meaning the fine hair of a newborn infant, and it indicated the fine hairs or down found on the young tea buds. "Orange" does not refer to color or flavor, but to the Netherlands' House of Orange. First used by Dutch merchants, the term was meant to convey the idea of noble quality. These leaves are rolled lengthwise and mixed with the golden tips of buds. The more buds, the more expensive the tea. OP usually has few buds included.

FOP, or flowery orange pekoe, is made from tender young leaves with the addition of a certain number of "tips," the ends of the young leaves, which are considered the highest-quality part of the leaf.

GFOP, golden flower orange pekoe, is considered a high-quality grade.

FTGFOP, or finest tippy golden flowery orange pekoe, is made using mostly tips. It makes a clear, light-amber-colored brew of very high quality.

SFTGFOP, or special finest tippy golden flowery orange pekoe, the highest grade, has a large quantity of leaves with golden tips. This is the highest-quality FOP.

P, pekoe, consists of the shorter leaves without tips, and is of low to medium quality.

"If you are cold, tea will warm you. If you are too heated, it will cool you. If you are depressed, it will cheer you. If you are excited, it will calm you."

—*William Gladstone (1809–1898), British prime minister*

FP, flowery pekoe, is made with leaves rolled into a round or ball shape, and is of medium quality.

PS, pekoe souchong, has shorter, coarser leaves of medium quality.

S, souchong, has large leaves rolled lengthwise, and is often used to make China smoked teas; souchong is of medium to high quality.

Broken Leaf

The same designations are used, with the addition of *B*, indicating broken. Broken-leaf teas are not inferior to whole leaf teas; the broken leaves just make the tea stronger. For example, broken orange pekoe is the finest broken-leaf tea and is designated BOP.

Fannings

Designated *BOPF*, fannings are small, flat pieces of broken orange pekoe leaves, used to make strong, robust teas. These teas are not of as high a quality as whole or broken leaf.

Dust

This is essentially the dregs left over from the tea process and includes bits of broken leaves. These are often used in tea bags. Dust is designated with a *D*—for example, BOPD for broken orange pekoe dust. Although CTC tea and dust have particles of about the same size, they have been produced differently. Dust is produced by the orthodox method, while CTC is the result of a mechanized process.

If you can't remember all that when you are at the tea store, just remember that the more letters (for example, SFTG-FOP), usually the higher the quality of the tea. In buying tea, as with buying many other things, you get what you pay for. Although cost should not be the final consideration, generally the higher-quality teas command higher prices. But taste is individual, and certainly the best for one person may be far from the best for another.

CHAPTER 2

History and Legend

"There is a great deal of poetry and fine sentiment
in a chest of tea."
—*Ralph Waldo Emerson (1803–1882)*

LEGENDARY BEGINNINGS

It all began with a single leaf, picked or pulled from a tree over five hundred thousand years ago. Why, on this particular day, did our prehistoric ancestors pull leaves off the tree that we now call *Camellia sinensis*, and put them into a vessel filled with hot water? Why did they choose that particular plant? Depending on whom you ask, it could be happy accident, divine plan, or the result of much trial and error. Fortunately for us, though, they did, and the results have changed the world forever.

It isn't often that scientific theory predates legend, but this is precisely what happens in the history of tea. K. Jelinek, editor of the *Illustrated Encyclopedia of Prehistoric Man* (1978), suggests that the first tea was consumed by the time of the early Paleolithic Period (about five hundred thousand years ago). Archeological evidence from that period indicates that leaves of *Camellia sinensis* (the source of all true tea, including white, green, oolong, and black) were placed in boiling water by *Homo erectus* in the area that is now China. The fact that the tea plant is indigenous to many parts of China supports Jelinek's claim.

In contrast, the most popular and best-known legend about the origin of tea dates to about 3000 BCE, during the time of the mythical Chinese emperor Shen Nung, who is said to be the first ever to taste tea.

According to Chinese mythology, Shen Nung was third in the sequence of divine monarchs called the Three August Ones, legendary rulers from whom all Chinese are said to have descended. The first of these rulers was Empress Nu Wa (also known as Nu-kya), mother of the Chinese people, who used yellow earth to create human beings in the image of gods. She was followed by Fu Xi (also known as Fu-Hsi), who brought knowledge of the Eight Diagrams that allowed the Chinese people to identify and follow heavenly decrees. The third ruler was Shen Nung.

The rule of the Three August Ones represents a special time in Chinese history, an era when ordinary Chinese people lived side by side with the gods. This legendary civilization, the Chinese believe, was the beginning of a people who were superior to all other beings, able to create a culture of unparalleled strength, wisdom, and longevity. Thus, in the earliest stages of Chinese history, the seeds were planted for conflicts that would prove devastating to Chinese civilization five thousand years later—conflicts instigated by the sale of tea. A civilization that believes it is rooted in the divine and that all other civilizations are inferior invites conflict from competition and sets the stage for war.

"God bless the man that
first discovered Tea!"
            —*Robert W. Service*
                (1874–1958)

But war and conflict were the antithesis of what Shen
Nung stood for, for his epithet was "Divine Healer." Scholars of Chinese mythology date the stories told about Shen
Nung to sometime between 2838 and 2698 BCE. He goes
by many other names as well, including Yen Ti, Earth
Emperor, Fire Emperor, Red Emperor, Divine Husbandman, and Divine Farmer.

Shen Nung is considered the father of traditional Chinese medicine, an ancient practice deeply rooted in Taoism
that encompasses the relationships among heaven, earth,
and man. His greatest contribution was to bring knowledge
of herbs and medicine to the people. Legend says that he
tested hundreds of herbs for their beneficial and harmful
effects.

The legend of Shen Nung's discovery of tea is an oft-told
tale, relating how this mythical emperor once stopped to
rest underneath a tea tree during a long journey. Known
for the care he took with sanitary matters, Shen Nung was

爐 鴻 車

A bamboo basket for firing tea, one of many types of utensils that were used for tea preparation during the T'ang dynasty; redrawn from an image in the *Ch'a Ching*, 780 CE

boiling water to drink before he continued on his way. As he sat there, a leaf from the tree above him floated down toward earth, but happened (as things often happen in myth and legend) to fall into his pot of hot water instead. The leaf colored the water, and Shen Nung guessed that something quite magical was happening. Carefully, he took the pot off the fire and, when it cooled, took a few sips of the liquid. As the beverage flowed through his veins, he was filled with a sense of peace and calm.

Of all Shen Nung's accomplishments and of all the herbs he was said to have tested and introduced to the world, it is his discovery of tea for which he is most famous and most revered. That leaf, accidentally drifting into a pot of boiling water, colored not merely the water, but events in China and in civilizations around the globe, bringing passion, peace, and contentment as well as addiction, war, and poverty. But it all began with a simple leaf.

CONFUSING TERMS IN EARLY RECORDS

As the story of Shen Nung illustrates, the beginning of humanity's experience of tea is "steeped" in myth and legend. In the search for an accurate, trustworthy account of tea's early days, the literature of the time seems a logical place to begin. But even there, uncertainty abounds.

There have been many attempts to determine the most ancient references to tea in Chinese literature, but scholars have not come to consensus. Part of the confusion arises from the fact that the ancient Chinese character used to designate tea was also used to refer to other shrubs and plants. A modern analogy would be our imprecise but common usage of the name "daisy" to refer to any number of flowers belonging to the Compositae, or "Daisy" family. Until the time of the T'ang dynasty (618–907 CE), the character *t'u* was used to refer to tea and other medicinal plants, in particular the plant sowthistle, *Sonchus arvensis*.

One of these early, confusing references occurs in the *Shijing* (*Book of Odes*), said to have been edited by Confucius (c. 550–478 BCE). The entry in question is in Ode Ten, "The Lament of a Discarded Wife," and reads, "Who says that t'u is bitter? It is as sweet as the tsi." The word *t'u*, which centuries later referred to tea, most probably referred to sowthistle during the age of Confucius. The word *tsi* was probably used to indicate the small plant shepherd's purse, *Capsella bursa-pastoris*.

Another mention of t'u dates to 50 BCE and is from a merchant, Wang Piu. His surviving written records include a conversation with a servant in which he speaks of buying (and then boiling) t'u while living in a village in the Szechwan district. The fact that this province, which encompasses the mountain Wutu, was thought to be the birthplace of cultivated tea lends credibility to the possibility that, here, t'u actually did refer to the tea shrub.

Tea is mentioned several times in *Shen Nung's Herbal Classic*, a compilation of writings named in honor of Shen Nung. Written during the Later Han dynasty (25–220 CE), several centuries after the legendary ruler was thought to have lived, the book, which includes information on an impressive 365 herbs, is called by many names, including *Shen-nong Ben-cao-jin* (*Classic of Herbal Medicine*), *Shen Husbandman*, *The Herbal Classic of the Divine Plowman*, and *Pharmacopoeia of the Heavenly Husbandman*. In actuality, the book was most probably written by many different authors.

Among the better-known passages referencing tea in *Shen Nung's Herbal Classic* is the following: "Bitter t'u is called ch'a, hsuan, and yu. It grows in winter in the valleys by the streams and on the hills of Ichow in the province of Szechwan and does not perish in severe winter. It is gathered on the third day of the month in April and then dried."

Although the references to tea from the *Herbal Classic* are mentioned frequently in popular literature (as proof that the popularity of tea dates back to times before the Common Era), they were probably not included in the original text, since the character *ch'a* was used in the book to reference tea, and this character did not come into usage

The strokes of the character *ch'a* are inscribed in the order set forth in the accompanying illustration; beginning at the top and writing downward, after the Chinese fashion.

From *All About Tea*, 1935

until the seventh century, a full 3,400 years after the time of Shen Nung, and anywhere from five hundred to seven hundred years after the first distribution of the book named in his honor.

EARLY REFERENCES TO TEA

Beginning in the third century CE, references to tea seem more credible, in particular those dating to the time of Hua T'o, a highly respected physician and surgeon. In his book *Shin Lun*, he wrote, "To drink bitter t'u constantly makes one think better," and this time t'u most probably referred to the plant we call tea today (*Camellia sinensis*).

Another example from this period comes from a letter written by Liu Kun, a general in the Ch'in dynasty (265–289 CE), to his nephew, Liu Yen, governor of Yenchow. In this letter, Liu Kun admitted that he felt aged and depressed and "wanted some real t'u." Since one of the earliest medicinal uses of tea was as a soothing, relaxing drink, this probably refers to tea.

Perhaps the best-known and most frequently mentioned of all early references to tea dates to 350 CE, when the Chinese scholar Kuo P'o wrote an annotated dictionary called the *Erh Ya Chu*. Kuo P'o calls tea *kia* (yet another name!) or "bitter tea," *k'u t'u*. He indicates that the "beverage is made from the leaves by boiling." Kuo P'o also writes, "The plant is as small as the gardenia and in winter has leaves which can be made into a drink. What is plucked early is called ch'a and what is plucked later is called ming, otherwise known as ch'uan which is called bitter tea by the people of Szechwan."

This mention of the word *ming* indicates knowledge of the importance of time or season of harvest. Other ancient writers also used the word to describe tea, including the fifth-century poet Pao Ling-hui, who mentioned the "fragrant ming."

EARLY MEDICINAL USES

By the fourth century, tea was a part of Chinese daily life. People did not drink it for pleasure, however, but continued to use it for its value as a medicine. Methods of processing the leaves to make a flavorful beverage were still in the far-off future, and the people of fourth- and fifth-century China had to struggle to get down the bitter brew. Lacking a "spoonful of sugar" to help the medicine go down, they tried masking the bitterness with all kinds of additives, including onions, ginger, salt, and orange. Apparently, these additives did little to make the brew palatable. In addition to being drunk, tea was also occasionally eaten like a vegetable, or even used as snuff or applied externally as a poultice.

Tea, as a bitter brew, was used to cure any number of things, including poor eyesight, fatigue, rheumatic pains, skin ailments (such as sores and ulcers), and problems with kidneys and lungs. It was also considered useful for keeping one alert and improving digestion. The authors of *Shen Nung's Herbal Classic* make it clear that tea was well respected as an important part of their pharmacopoeia, claiming that it would alleviate problems caused by tumors, bladder problems, and sores or abscesses about the head. Drinking tea was more than a cure. It is clear that the authors of the *Herbal Classic* believed that drinking tea did much to prevent illness—and social problems as well!: "Habitual drinking can ease the mind and benefit the qi, increase stamina and keep one fresh and young. . . . Tea is better than wine for it leadeth not to intoxication, neither does it cause a man to say foolish things and repent thereof in his sober moments. It is better than water for it does not carry disease; neither does it act like poison as water does when it contains foul and rotten matter."

The latter statement is undoubtedly true, because the water for tea was always boiled, ridding it of many disease-bearing organisms.

A stone grinding mill for tea, used during the T'ang dynasty; redrawn from an image in the *Ch'a Ching*, 780 CE

THE FIRST CULTIVATION OF TEA

Tea was indisputably valued as medicine in the latter part of the fourth century and during the fifth century. The increased use naturally created a greater demand for the leaves, which was met by harvesting leaves from the wild and, eventually, by cultivating the tea plant.

Wild tea plants in southwestern China grew quite tall, making harvesting difficult. Farmers and peasants solved this problem, at least in the short term, by simply cutting the trees down to get the fresh leaves. This practice continued until it became obvious that it would soon deplete whole forests of tea trees, and a primitive silviculture was initiated around the middle of the fourth century. Farmers observed that tea plants grew well in gravelly soils that had good drainage, and they duplicated those conditions for cultivating tea.

The first tea cultivation probably occurred in the hill district of Szechwan, where the trees were planted on hillsides. Planters today, like their counterparts 1,700 years ago, know the value of well-drained soils, and in many places around the world, tea shrubs are still planted on hillsides, where drainage is excellent.

During the time of the Northern Wei Dynasty (386– 535 CE), tea leaves were at least primitively processed, and, presumably, the taste improved. A dictionary of this period states that in the district between the provinces of Hupeh and Szechwan, tea leaves were harvested, made into cakes, and roasted until hard and reddish in color. The cakes were then pounded into small pieces and placed in a chinaware pot. This may be the first indication of the unrelenting quest for the best processing methods to produce the best-tasting teas, a quest that we continue even today.

During the Southern Dynasty (420–478 CE), the cultivation of tea was common, and it was considered a valuable crop. During this time, the imperial court demanded that a tea tribute be paid by the peasants. The writer Shan Ch'ien-Chih reported that "Twenty lis [a li is a little over 700 yards] west from the city of Wucheng, in the province of Chekiang, there is the Wen mountain, on which grows the tea reserved to the emperor as tribute tea."

This first tribute was a precursor of tea taxes that were to have repercussions for many cultures around the world.

BUDDHISM AND TEA:
THE LEGEND OF PRINCE BODHIDHARMA

The early history of tea centers around China, even though the tea plant (in varying forms) is indigenous to both southwestern China and the Assam region of India (and many other places in southeastern Asia). It is puzzling that the Chinese made such thorough use of the plant, from the days of antiquity, while the Indians did not. There are few references to the use of tea in India until about the sixth century, and even then, usage of the plant was not widespread. It is during this period, however, that one of the most famous of all legends about tea is said to have occurred. It happened like this:

Prince Bodhidharma (also known as Pu Tai Ta-Mo in Chinese, and Daruma Daishi in Japanese) grew up near Madras, India, in the Sardilli family, in the fifth century. He was a wealthy and favored young prince. When he was a young man, he came upon the teachings of Buddha and thereafter dedicated his life to study and meditation. He studied for many years and became so skilled and knowledgeable that, in 470, he was asked to travel to China to reintroduce Buddhism. (Buddhism had reached China 600 years before this time, but had begun to die out there.) It is known that Bodhidharma traveled first to Canton in 470 and that in 520 he traveled to northern China, where he was granted an interview with the Liang emperor, Wu-Ti. This emperor was noted for his good works and was eager to speak with Bodhidharma, for he felt sure that the monk would tell him that he was well on his way to enlightenment. When Bodhidharma said that enlightenment could not be obtained through merit, Wu-Ti apparently was not pleased and left the interview in great confusion.

Leaving the emperor, Bodhidharma went to Loyang, crossed the Yang-tse River, then traveled up into the mountains of the Sung range to stay at the Shaolin temple. Legend says that to fulfill a vow, he spent nine years in meditation in a small cave there. It is from this long meditation that many of the legends about Bodhidharma—and tea—originate.

Some versions of the legend say that Bodhidharma was looking at a wall in a cave for nine years, while others suggest that he simply vowed to do without sleep, giving his

Bodhidharma (from a drawing by Kaempfer, 1692)

full attention to the meditation of Buddha. According to this version, after five years, his need for sleep became overpowering, and in desperation to keep himself awake, he pulled leaves off a nearby bush and began chewing on them. Fortunately for him—and for us—or perhaps it was divinely ordained—the leaves came off a tea bush and were simultaneously stimulating and soothing, immediately reviving him. He used the leaves of this shrub over and over again until he was able to complete his vow.

Once the vow was complete, Bodhidharma is said to have turned his attention to helping the monks of the temple. Not only did he introduce them to tea, to enable them to stay awake during long periods of meditation, but he also taught them physical techniques to strengthen the body to withstand the rigors of sitting long hours of meditation. This physical practice, also used as a form of self-defense against bandits and invading war lords, eventually grew into the martial arts style called kung fu.

Like many legends, this one has endless variations and inconsistencies. After all, as previously indicated, there are written records of tea being drunk for centuries preceding the arrival of Bodhidharma in China. In some versions, the prince actually fell asleep during the years of his vow and was so disgusted with himself when he woke that he pulled off his eyelids so that they would never again close. Where he tossed these aside, the tea shrub began to grow. (The popular "eyebrow" tea, *chun mee-cha*, introduced in 1958, has nothing to do with this eyelid legend, but instead refers to the curved "eyebrow" shape of the processed leaf.)

Wherever tea actually originated, it was used as an aid to meditation among the Buddhist monks of Bodhidharma's time. Because it was such an important meditation tool, and because meditation was such an essential part of the type of Buddhism that Bodhidharma preached (now known as Zen Buddhism), the spread of tea parallels the spread of Buddhism from China to other places in Asia.

CHAPTER 3

Tea in Ancient China and Korea

"Its liquor is like the sweetest dew of heaven."

—Lu Yu, eighth-century tea master

TEA IN THE T'ANG DYNASTY

The imperial court of the T'ang dynasty (618–907) enjoyed great power and influence and controlled vast lands and wealth. A contributing factor to this expansion of power was a series of interconnecting canals that allowed communication and transportation to all parts of the empire and beyond. Boats on the canals carried tea and other consumer goods from one port to another, and as foreign trade grew, the empire expanded.

Of course, Chinese traders used other means of transportation as well, and wherever Chinese traders went, tea went with them. At this point in history, tea leaves were pressed into a brick or cake, then baked until hard. This gave them a long shelf life and made them easy to transport. To make tea from a brick of baked leaves, one broke off a portion of the hard cake, ground it into powder with a mortar and pestle, then boiled it for several minutes to make tea, which was poured into a bowl.

As processing methods evolved from raw leaf to baked brick, the taste improved accordingly, and tea enjoyed a surge of popularity throughout China during the T'ang dynasty. Tea was served not only at the imperial court, but almost everywhere else as well. Drinking tea soon became an essential part of everyday life for many people, from emperors to peasants. At this time, the tea drunk in China was green tea. The Chinese did not drink black tea until they began to process it for export to the West, beginning in the seventeenth century.

Those who could afford it drank only the finest teas, which at that time came from the regions of Xiashou, Guangzhou, and Huzhon and offered a complexity of flavors. Eventually, social status became associated with the type of tea one drank (or could afford). Not only did the tea itself have to meet high standards, but everything associated with it—the utensils, bowls, water, and tea caddy—all had to be of the finest quality.

The T'ang dynasty, which proved to be one of the greatest in China history, valued quality and beauty. It was a time of great sophistication, characterized by a love of learning and the arts. Poetry, painting, calligraphy, music, and landscape gardening all enjoyed popularity during this time, and inevitably, this environment of refinement influenced the culture of tea.

Naturally, people needed a place to get a bowl of tea, and teahouses and tea gardens soon sprang up in cities and towns across the empire. Many of these tea gardens became manifestations of the sophistication and refinement of the T'ang culture. Along with the search for the best teas came the development of the tea master, one who could find the highest-grade tea leaves from growers in the various

Lu Yu

regions, and who could prepare the most delicious teas. Tea masters were in great demand, particularly among the royalty and high officials.

LU YU, FIRST TEA MASTER

Of all the tea masters who lived during the T'ang dynasty, Lu Yu was the best known, so famous, in fact, that he has been called the "father of tea," "deity of tea," "sage of tea," and the "immortal of tea."

Although there is some question as to the exact date and place of his birth, Lu Yu was probably born in the district of Chin Ling some time between 728 and 733. There are countless stories and legends about him, most of which say that he was abandoned as a baby and adopted by the Buddhist monk Zhiji, spending his early years in the monastery.

In spite of the surroundings of his youth, however, Lu Yu proved to be temperamentally unfit for the life of the priesthood. He was in a state of constant rebellion that caused the monks to punish him by assigning him difficult and menial tasks. The monks hoped that as Lu Yu performed these tasks, he would learn the necessary discipline and humility to continue with his priestly studies, but it was all to no avail. At the age of thirteen, Lu Yu ran away to join an opera troupe and fulfill his dream of becoming a clown. He seemed perfectly suited to this life and delighted audiences wherever he went, playing the fool and making people laugh.

In spite of his restlessness, however, Lu Yu exhibited an unusually keen intellect, and he soon became bored with performing with the troupe. Although he did not miss the austerity and simplicity of the life of the monks, he did miss his life as a student. Fortunately, one of Lu Yu's greatest admirers was an official who became aware of the young man's intellectual yearnings. His patronage allowed Lu Yu to further his education by studying the ancient writings while he continued with his profession.

Then, in 760, an armed rebellion forced Lu Yu to leave the district where he was performing with the opera troupe. Along with many others, he took refuge in the village of Huzhou, in present-day Zhejiang Province—an unexpected turn of events that proved to be fortunate for this clown-turned-scholar. Among other things, the climate of this region was perfect for growing tea. The weather was warm, there was plenty of moisture, and the ground was rich and fertile. Tea gardens and teahouses were in abundance.

Like other young men, Lu Yu was attracted to the teahouses, where, as was the custom of the day, men gathered. These establishments throughout the country were places where friends and scholars came together, not only to drink and talk about tea, but also to discuss art and listen to music. In the best teahouses, the air was perfumed with rare incense and flowers, and only the finest teas were served. In such an atmosphere, one could relax and enjoy the most subtle nuances of aesthetic pleasures, including an appreciation for the taste of the best-quality teas.

After a time, Lu Yu became friendly with a man named Jiao Ran, who owned one of the teahouses of the Zhejiang region, and before long Lu Yu grew fascinated, then obsessed, with tea. It was here in the teahouse of his friend that he found the perfect outlet for his scholarly ambition. He was soon not only running the teahouse for Jiao Ran, but also learning as much as he possibly could about tea.

Lu Yu's Tea Classic

Tea became the focus of Lu Yu's life. He was relentless in his quest to learn everything there was to know about tea. The result of this consuming passion was the three-volume, ten-part book called *Ch'a Ching*, the *Tea Classic*, published in 780.

The book deals with the following aspects of tea:

1. Origin of the tea plant
2. Tools for gathering the leaves
3. Production and manipulation of the leaves
4. Description of the twenty-four implements necessary to serve and enjoy tea
5. How to make a cup of tea (methods of infusion)
6. Rules for drinking tea
7. Historical summary of tea and its usage
8. Sources of tea, plantations, and so forth
9. Nonessential tools
10. Illustrations of tea utensils

Farmers and agriculturists interested in learning to cultivate tea found an unlikely hero in Lu Yu, the man who'd gone from monk to clown to scholar to tea master. With an increased demand for tea came a corresponding demand for information about how to grow it. Although tea had been cultivated in the Szechwan district for hundreds of years, by the mid-tenth century, the practice of growing tea had spread through the Yangtze Valley and along the coast as well. With a growing market, farmers planted tea wherever they could find a patch of land, and by this time, tea cultivation was common and widespread. Nonetheless, knowledge about how to grow the plants and harvest the leaves was still spread only by word of mouth, passed from one generation to the next or from one neighbor to another.

There was a resulting need for information about how

A page from the *Ch'a Ching*,
the *Tea Classic*, 780 CE

to propagate and care for tea plants, how to prune the
shrubs, harvest the leaves—in short, how to take tea from
a shrub to a valuable commodity. In his *Tea Classic*, Lu Yu
provided this information in written, accessible form.

The work begins with a description of the tea plant and
its habitat. Lu Yu reports that tea plants growing naturally
on the hills and beside the streams in the province of Szechwan are "sometimes so big that it takes two men to encir-
cle them with their arms." He goes on to say that the
flowers of the tea plant are like "white cinnamon roses"
and the seeds similar to those of the coconut palm. After
describing the plant, he offers advice as to the best places
to grow it: The most favorable is in "the soil of disintegrated
stones," the next best is where gravel is present, and the
least favorable soil is yellow clay.

As for taste, Lu Yu decidedly prefers the leaves of the wild plants to those of trees growing in "confined spaces"—a comparison impossible for modern tea drinkers to make, since any wild tea trees that may still exist are extremely rare. During Lu Yu's lifetime, cultivation of tea was not, of course, as widespread as it is today.

He advises tea growers to pick the new shoots, which he thinks are better than buds (in contrast to modern growers, who cherish the buds), and he considers the curled leaf tips to be superior to those that are uncurled.

The Tea Classic offers specific advice for harvesting the leaves, suggesting that harvest take place only when the weather is clear. Tea leaves four or five inches long should be picked during March, April, or May. Perhaps the following is the best-known quote from *The Tea Classic*: "The best quality leaves must have creases like the leathern boot of Tartar horsemen, curl like the dewlap of a mighty bullock, unfold like a mist rising out of a ravine, gleam like a lake touched by a zephyr, and be wet and soft like fine earth newly swept by rain."

Lu Yu's masterful work covers the full spectrum of tea in Chinese culture. In Part Five, he says, "After baking . . . [the tea brick] should be put in a paper bag so that it will not lose its fragrant flavor" (a clear indication that paper bags were in use in China during the eighth century!). Much of his impressive expertise at preparing tea concerns the careful selection of water. One oft-told story is that Lu Yu could determine from a cup of tea precisely where the water to make it was collected—either along the shore of

事 從 宗

A brush used in the T'ang dynasty for the removal of dust during tea preparation; redrawn from an image in the *Ch'a Ching*, 780 CE

a river or midstream. As for his water preference for tea, he says the water from a mountain spring is best, then the water from a river, while the water from a well is of the lowest quality.

Lu Yu's explanation of how to determine the best water temperature for making tea is nearly poetic: "When the water first boils, there appears something like the eyes of fishes on the surface, and a little noise can be heard. Then appears something like a spring rushing forth and a string of pearls at the side, this is the second boiling." The tea, which has been broken off the baked brick and ground into a powder, is added to the water after the "second boiling." The appearance of the "waves and breakers" is called the third boiling. A dipper full of cold water is added at this point, to "revive the youth of the water" and to enhance the flavor of the boiling tea. If the tea is left in the pot after the third boiling, it is considered "overboiled," and Lu Yu advises against using it, if one wants superior taste.

Part Six gives instructions for drinking, and begins with the statement that all beings, including birds and animals, have to drink to live. Lu Yu suggests that this is what water is for, and that wine is used to drown sorrows, but that tea is drunk to avoid sleepiness.

Tea should be drunk, according to Lu Yu, four or five times a day for those who are "depressed, suffering from headache, eye-ache, fatigue of the four limbs or pains in the joints." He also writes that bitter tea, combined with the roots of small onions, is good for "children who are frightened and tumble without apparent causes."

Although many people were still adding spices and other exotic ingredients to tea, Lu Yu's clear preference for superior taste (tumbling children notwithstanding) is to add nothing except a little salt, which is put in after the first boiling. As he puts it in the sixth section, "Sometimes onion, ginger, jujube, orange peel and peppermint are used, and it is permitted to boil for some time before skimming off the froth. Alas! This is the slop water of a ditch."

The fourth section of the *Ch'a Ching* is dedicated to the twenty-four implements needed for the preparation of tea. This has been called Lu Yu's Tea Code and is a precursor for the creation of the tea ceremony, first in China, then later, and more significantly, in Japan. Famous for his attention to detail, Lu Yu gives precise measurements for each of the implements used, including an "all-in-one" basket "one foot five inches high, two feet four inches long and two feet wide," used to hold the implements needed to prepare tea.

The eighteenth implement that Lu Yu discusses is the china cup. He suggests that those from Yueh Chou are best, clearly preferring the beautiful blue celadon glaze that

A lacquer cup holder, commonly used during the T'ang dynasty to avoid burning the hands; redrawn from an image in the *Ch'a Ching*, 780 CE

characterizes cups made in the North. He suggests that these give the beverage a beneficial greenish cast. White cups, he goes on to say, give the tea a pinkish cast that he considers distasteful.

Such attention to details may seem excessive to Westerners today, but Lu Yu lived during a time when Confucianism, Buddhism, and Taoism were all prevalent. Each of these paths was rich in symbolism and involved a deep spiritual practice. As Kakuzo Okakura, Japanese scholar and curator of Japanese art at Boston's Museum of Fine Arts, put it in his 1906 work, *The Book of Tea*, "The pantheistic symbolism of the time was urging one to mirror the Universal in the Particular." It was one of Lu Yu's greatest gifts that he found the means of expressing universal harmony and order within the particulars of preparing and serving a bowl of tea.

After Lu Yu had published the *Ch'a Ching*, he enjoyed enormous popularity, attracting attention both from peasants, who had heard stories of his mastery, and from the royal court. He and Emperor Taisung (763–779) eventually became friends. In spite of his popularity, however, Lu Yu remained restless and dissatisfied. Ironically, toward the end of his life, he sought out an almost monastic lifestyle that provided solitude, quiet, and time for contemplation and meditation.

Inevitably, Lu Yu had his own followers. Perhaps the most famous of his disciples was a poet by the name of Lu Tung (also seen as Lo Tung), who lived during the late T'ang dynasty and wrote at length of tea. One of his poems declares that the first cup merely moistened his lips and throat, but the second cup broke his loneliness, and by the fifth cup he was purified. The "sixth cup calls me to the realms of the immortals. The seventh cup—ah, but I could take no more." Perhaps his most famous line is, "I am in no way interested in immortality, but only in the taste of tea," a quote that is used frequently and enthusiastically by tea merchants even today.

THE IMPERIAL TEA TRIBUTE

Lu Yu's work created a surge in the popularity of tea that resulted in more successful methods of tea cultivation and processing in many regions of T'ang dynasty China.

During this period, the finest tea grew in Yang-Hsien, a mountainous region near present-day Shanghai. In the late 770s, an envoy from the emperor was sent there to determine just why this mountainous region produced such superior tea. While there, he was given a bowl of tea, which he considered the finest he had ever tasted. The envoy immediately sent 28,000 grams (1,000 ounces) of this tea back to court. As soon as he tasted it, the emperor demanded that he be sent some of this tea every year. The demand for tribute paid with tea, which had actually begun in the fifth century, was to have tremendously beneficial results for the

Tea's Influence on Chinese Ceramics

The popularity of tea, aided by the huge fame of Lu Yu's book, had a great impact on the ceramics and pottery industry of the time. Sophisticated artists created more and more elaborate ceramics for holding tea. At one time, craftsmen had used gold and silver in the ceramics, but the tea masters discouraged this practice, claiming that the use of metal ruined the taste of the tea.

During the T'ang dynasty, the tea cups or bowls were called *wan* and were classified according to the color of the glaze and how it influenced the color of the tea infusion. The first mention of

Chinese porcelain outside China is from an Arab traveler, Soleiman, who wrote an account of his journey into China during the mid-ninth century. He reported, "They have in China a very fine clay with which they make vases which are as transparent as glass. Water is seen through them."

The finest of these tea bowls were not only beautiful to look at, but also made a beautiful ringing sound when tapped lightly. Poets of the day referred to them as "disks of thinnest ice," or "tilted lotus leaves floating upon a stream."

imperial Chinese economy over the years—and devastating results for the farmers and peasants.

During harvest time, usually in April, girls were sent to the mountainsides to pick the leaves. Picking ceased at noon. During the afternoons, the entire village worked to cook, powder, and press the tea into a paste that was then baked into cakes.

Even though the tea-making period only lasted a month in this mountainous region, it coincided with the time when the rice fields needed to be planted. Because the peasants were forced to neglect their own fields at this critical time, the rice and vegetable harvest was always severely depleted. The result was real hunger, and even famine later in the year.

The tribute created even greater hardship for the peasants and growers as more and more tea was demanded. During some years, thousands of catties (one catty equals twenty to twenty-one ounces) were demanded from a single region. And each year, it seemed, land in more and more regions was demanded for growing tea. Most of the tribute tea sent to court was sold to traders to boost the economy. Unfortunately, the peasants working in the tea gardens were not allowed to benefit from these sales individually, as private trade was forbidden. The very choicest tea was saved for the Son of Heaven—the name given to the Chinese emperor—and for the members of his court and family.

Tea's prominence, not only as a valuable commodity but also as an integral part of the Buddhist practice, helped it spread from one end of China to the other. But the fate of tea was closely tied to the fate of Buddhism, and when Buddhism began to lose favor with the government and court toward the latter part of the T'ang dynasty, tea, too, began to slip in popularity. As the power of the T'ang dynasty began to wane, Buddhists were persecuted, and 4,600 Buddhist temples fell to government proscription. It was, perhaps, a signal of the times that were to come. The T'ang dynasty ended in 907 when Tatars invaded, and for several decades, China was ruled by the Tatars. Tea, ceramics, scholarship, and many other essential elements of Chinese culture were, for the time being, abandoned.

TEA IN THE SONG DYNASTY

In 960 the country once again came under Chinese rule when Zhao Huangyin (927–976) became emperor and began the Song (also seen as Sung) dynasty. This dynasty was almost as splendid and refined as the T'ang, and tea once again played an important role in both the economy and the culture of the Chinese, from the peasant to the emperor.

It was during this dynastic age that enthusiasm and praise for tea reached a fever pitch. Lichihlai, a Song poet, said that the three most deplorable things in the world were: "the spoiling of fine youth through false education, the degradation of fine paintings through vulgar admiration, and the utter waste of fine tea through incompetent manipulation."

Not surprisingly, the amount of imperial tribute tea demanded by the emperor paralleled the rise of tea's popularity. Not only did he require vast amounts of tea to be sent to court, he also specified how the tea should be picked.

At the beginning of the Song dynasty, most of the tea used for tribute came from Fujian Province on China's southeastern coast. The finest of this tea was thought to come from Pei-Yuan, one of forty-six tea gardens in the region. The leaves of this superior tea were gathered in the "time of the Excited Insects" (March), and the court rules for harvesting, or "plucking," were detailed and strict. The leaves had to be picked while still covered with dew, meaning early morning. Only young girls were allowed to pluck the leaves, and their fingernails had to be kept just the right length, because the leaves were plucked with the nails, not the fingers. This kept the leaves from being contaminated with sweat and body heat. The picked leaves were then placed in a basket that the girls carried on their backs.

The emperor himself, Hui Tsung, who ruled from 1101 to 1125, greatly contributed to the popularity of tea, as he spent much of his fortune and almost all of his time in writing about, tasting, and searching for the best teas available. This Son of Heaven (which is what the Chinese called their emperors) lived in isolation and wrote a book on tea, called *Ta Kuan Ch'a Lun* (also seen as *Guan Ch'a Lun*), which was well respected by the tea masters of the age. It became the essential guide for tea during his lifetime.

He wrote that it was important to learn to determine the values of different teas, which "vary as much in appearance as do the faces of men." In this book he stipulated—taking the demands of earlier emperors one step further—that tea for the emperor should be picked by young virgins wearing gloves. He dictated that only the bud and the first leaf should be picked. These were put on a golden platter to dry in the sun before being processed to make the emperor's tea. Even the diet of the young girls who plucked the leaves was restricted. They were forbidden certain kinds of meats and fish so that impurities in their breath would not affect the fragrance of the tea.

What constituted the finest tea? It was a matter of choice, but like wine that is universally appreciated, some teas

White Tea

White tea was considered one of the rarest of all the twenty kinds of tea discussed in the *Ta Kuan Chá Lun*. According to this twelfth-century book, white tea comes from tea trees with widely spreading branches that grow on forested mountainsides. The emperor suggested that the best leaves were those "whitish in color shaped like sparrows' tongues." So rare was this tea that it was only found in three or four different tea gardens, and a total of only two to three bags full of the leaves were collected each year. (White tea remains relatively rare and quite expensive, even today. It is classified as "white" because of the way the leaves are processed.)

exhibit characteristics, such as color, clarity, and sweet fragrance, that are considered superior by all. During this period, tea leaves were classified according to their size and age—the youngest leaves being the new buds, the oldest being the larger leaves. The smallest buds were thought to be priceless, while the larger, older leaves were used to make a low-grade tea drunk by the peasants and lower classes.

Of course, only the buds and smallest leaves were processed to make tea for the emperor. One tea, called "Small-Leaf Dragon," was made with the freshest buds, which were crushed and molded into a cake that weighed only one and a half ounces, but sold for two ounces of gold! At this point, some tea was literally more valuable, ounce for ounce, than gold. In contrast, large, low-grade tea leaves were molded into bricks and cakes and used for trade and export, but no matter how coarse and bitter the tea, there was a steady demand for tea from China.

THE TEA AND HORSE CARAVAN ROAD

During the Song dynasty, tea became more and more important as an item of trade with tribes living on the fringe of the empire. People throughout the empire and beyond its borders wanted tea. The Mongol, the Tatar, the Turk, and the Tibetan all wanted processed tea leaves that they could brew into a drink that was not only good for them but that, increasingly, tasted good as well. Mongolians traded horses, wool, and musk for tea, but their thirst for tea became nearly insatiable. The Chinese court realized what power they held with their control of tea, and they began to manipulate these far-off tribes with the ebb and flow of tea. If Mongolian tribes were considered trouble-some to the imperial court, tea was simply withheld from them until they became more cooperative.

Horses proved to be the most valuable item needed by the Songs, and unimaginable amounts of tea were traded to the Tibetans for them. But just as desperately as the Song warriors wanted horses, the Tibetan tribes wanted tea.

Because the Tibetans lived at such high elevations, it was difficult for them to grow vegetables, and their diet was restricted by their geography. When tea became available, they boiled it in water, then mixed it with yak milk and butter to create a drink that provided desperately needed calories while adding some slight vegetative material to their animal-based diet.

According to the Tibetan book *Historic Collection of the Han and Tibet* (*Han Zang shi ji*), there is evidence that

"Picture you upon my knee,
Just tea for two, and two for tea."
—*Irving Caesar (1895–1996),
lyricist*

Tibetans were drinking tea at least as early as the Tubo regime (the same period as the T'ang dynasty).

There still exists today an ancient road, built during the Song dynasty, which is called the Tea and Horse Caravan Road. On this, traders traveled between Tibet and the Yunnan and Szechwan regions of China, taking tea from China and trading it mainly for horses from Tibet and other regions. Trade between the countries was so important that in 1074 the Chinese government established a Tea and Horse office. The *Historic Collection of the Han and Tibet* says that as many as twenty thousand war-horses from Tibetan tribes were exchanged for tea in a single year, and that up to 15,000,000 kilograms (33,069,000 pounds) of tea produced in Szechwan were taken to Tibet in a year.

It was on this well-established and well-used trade route that tea pressed into bricks proved to be of great value. The bricks, made in China, were carried by camel or yak caravans into Tibet. They were of uniform size and weight—about twenty centimeters (eight inches) by twenty-five centimeters (ten inches) by three centimeters (one inch)—and were usually embossed with Chinese characters or scenes. Tea bricks were so commonly accepted as currency in Tibet that sometimes horses and swords were priced according to the number of tea bricks they would bring.

Even today, Tibetans use tea that has been pressed into bricks. Just as in ancient times, small portions of the brick are carved off, then ground into a powder. This is boiled in water, then strained, and the infusion is mixed with yak milk, butter, and salt, put into a kettle and kept warm.

The tea and horse trade between Tibet and China was a mutually beneficial exchange that lasted for generations and peaked during the Ming dynasty.

TEA IN KOREA

While the Tibetans valued tea for dietary reasons, the Koreans embraced the drinking of tea for more spiritual reasons. They, too, found that drinking tea produced a state of alertness that lasted for long periods of time, which was a great boon for meditation.

Although many scholars date the beginning of drinking tea in Korea as far back as the end of the fourth century, by most accounts, Koreans began to drink tea during the sixth and seventh centuries. In reality, tea probably came to Korea, as it did to many other places, with the Buddhist monks. Many Korean scholars went to China during the Unified Silla period (668–935) to study Buddhism or Taoism, and returned home ready to share their experiences. One of these experiences was drinking tea as an aid to meditation. The mild stimulation of tea helped keep the practitioners awake during the long hours of required meditation.

Wherever tea came from, records indicate that during the time of Unified Silla, it was used as medicine and also as an offering to Buddha for ceremonial or social occasions. Even though today only water is offered in rituals, remnants of the ancient tea customs linger in Korea. The written character used to designate the special water utilized in death ceremonies and other Buddhist rituals is the same one used for tea. During the eighth century in Korea, tea and Buddhism were so closely aligned that even public teahouses sometimes displayed a statue of Buddha. Scholars and aristocrats would sit at these establishments to drink tea and discuss the teachings of Buddha.

The state called Koryo (918–1392) was established by Wang Kon, a ruler who held tea in great esteem. In spring, Wang Kon traveled to tea gardens throughout the region to help tend the tea plants. This was probably more a political gesture than a contribution of any actual labor, but it served as a good example to the people and showed his support of the tea industry.

Tea gradually became an important part of Korean culture and was drunk at special occasions, including weddings, the death of a parent, during commemoration of ancestors, or simply when one was welcoming guests. During Wang Kon's rule, people of different classes drank tea for different reasons. Commoners drank tea ceremonially to honor their ancestors. Aristocrats drank tea hoping to develop a sense of harmony. Monks drank tea to bring the mind to peace and equanimity. It was said that a senior monk watched how the novices drank their tea, and in this way determined their level of understanding of Buddhism.

After Wang Kon died, there was a great decline in the popularity of Buddhism throughout the country. Tea had been so closely associated with Buddhism that as the popularity of one declined, the other followed, although the monks continued to drink it in the monasteries. With fewer and fewer people drinking tea, most of the tea gardens in Korea were either destroyed or allowed to go into a state of disuse, except in the most remote southern regions of the peninsula, where many tea plantations were left intact.

THE SECOND SCHOOL OF TEA

During the middle of the eleventh century, the process of creating tea underwent a dramatic change in China as tea masters discovered new ways of processing tea leaves to bring forth enhanced flavor. Instead of being pounded and formed into bricks, tea leaves were dried and powdered, then boiling water was added, and the brew was whipped with a bamboo whisk until foamy. The resulting beverage was called "whipped tea," and the taste was decidedly superior. It was sometimes poetically called "frothy jade" because of its green color and the foamy appearance caused by the whipping motion. Because the flavor was so much better, this new method of preparation proved to be a monumental step in the development of tea. This type of green tea (which we call matcha today) is still used in the Japanese tea ceremony.

This new whipped tea formed what tea scholars call the "second phase" of tea. During the first phase, brick tea was the most common form of processed tea, and during the third phase, which we're still in today, tea lovers began steeping loose tea leaves in hot water. The three "schools" or "phases" of tea are Brick, Whipped, and Steeped, based on the most commonly used preparation method.

Many of the implements that had been used to make tea from bricks became obsolete when whipped or powdered tea came into fashion. Also, not surprisingly, the process suitable for making tea into a powder was different from the processes that were best for baking into a brick, meaning the "best" teas had changed.

Ceramics and pottery in China changed along with this new development. As the process for making tea changed from boiling pieces shaved from a brick to whipping a powder with hot water, different vessels were needed to brew and drink tea as well. The tea bowl, common during the T'ang dynasty, was replaced with a wide ceramic saucer.

The most famous tea vessels were those made in Fujian Province. These were dark with everted rims, glazed with black streaks and white speckles, and sometimes marked with characteristic brown drops that ran down the sides of the vessel. Tea masters prized these dark bowls highly because they showed the light yellowish-green liquid of the tea. Though called "purple," the bowls were actually a deep red and were made from the native clay. These pots were sometimes called "hare's fur cups" or "partridge cups" because the decoration resembled either the fur of the common hare or the plumage of the partridge. Fujian tea bowls were thick and heavy and kept the beverage hot for a long time.

Emperor Hui Tsung wrote, "The best kinds of chien [bowls] are very dark blue—almost black. They should be relatively deep so that the surface of the liquid will attain a milky color, and also rather wide to allow for whipping with a bamboo whisk." The whisk, he went on to say, should be "heavy, the brush like slivers of light, their tips sharp as swords. Then when the whisk is used there are not likely to be too many bubbles."

Teahouses were common in both the cities and villages. The most sophisticated of these were places of ease, comfort, and culture, famous for their sweet incense, beautiful floral arrangements, and decorative scrolls. In addition to tea, an alcoholic beverage made from plum blossoms was also served, along with small edible treats. Games were played to determine the best teas: Competitors would place a bit of tea powder into each cup, add boiling water, and whip the infusion with a bamboo whisk. After the powder settled to the bottom of the cup, the tea was drunk, and more hot water was poured over the used powder. This process was repeated as long as possible. The more cups of water the tea could color, the better the quality of the tea.

CHAPTER 4

Tea in Ancient Japan

"If a man has no tea in him, he is incapable
of understanding truth and beauty."

—Japanese proverb

THE DRINKING OF TEA, which was to have such a monumental impact on Japanese culture, began there as it did in
other places, in a small and modest way. It was, perhaps,
initiated by a simple sharing of a bowl of tea between two
scholars. At the end of the sixth century, China and Japan
enjoyed a close cultural exchange, and many Japanese
scholars went to China to study. They were greatly influenced by Chinese civilization in all areas, including art,
literature, calligraphy, science, and spiritual teachings.

TEA AND THE EARLY BUDDHIST MONKS

During the reign of Prince Shotoku (574–622) in Japan,
Japanese scholars showed a great interest in Buddhism.
Many of the Japanese scholars who went to China for religious studies also learned to cultivate tea, and eventually
brought back both tea seeds and the knowledge of how to
plant them and care for the plants. Because tea in China
during this period (corresponding to the T'ang dynasty)
was still baked into bricks, then chopped, ground, and

boiled in water, this is how the Japanese began making tea as well.

The Japanese emperor Shomu was instrumental in spreading tea's popularity, particularly among Buddhist monks. The story goes that, in 729, he gathered a group of one hundred monks for a day of reading Buddhist sacred scriptures. After the readings and meditations, he served the monks the new beverage, tea. This was a costly undertaking, as tea was one of the more expensive items brought from China at this time. The impact of this first Japanese tea party was considerable. The monks were so impressed with the effects of the beverage that they became obsessively interested in growing tea plants in their own country. One of the monks, Gyoki (658–749), dedicated the rest of his life to this pursuit, during which he built forty-nine temples and planted tea shrubs at each one.

In 794, the fiftieth emperor of Japan, Kammu, built an imperial palace called Capital of Peace, in Hei-an-kyo (now Kyoto). A tea garden was built within the walls of this palace, and a government caretaker was hired to tend it. This position was put under the auspices of the Medical Bureau, a clear indication that tea at this point in Japan's history was still an important medicine.

Once begun, the flow of tea through Japan seemed unstoppable. In 805, the most famous of all early Japanese tea enthusiasts went to China to study, and returned carrying seeds of the tea plant. Saicho (better known by the name awarded him after his death—Dengyo Daishi) planted these seeds at Mount Hiei in the province of Omi.

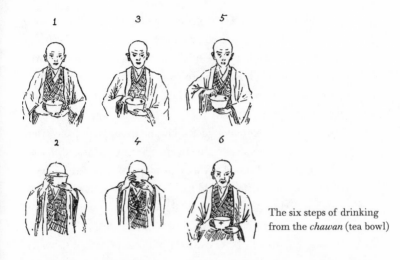

The six steps of drinking
from the *chawan* (tea bowl)

Even today, there is a tea garden on this site, some twelve
hundred years after the original tea garden was built.

Toward the end of the ninth century, relations between
Japan and China became strained, and Japanese diplomatic
missions were abolished. Along with everything else Chinese, the popularity of tea declined sharply for the next
three hundred years, except in the monasteries. During this
period, Japan continued to develop and strengthen its own
traditions, rather than mimic those of China.

ZEN AND THE ART OF TEA

In the twelfth century, renewed relations between Japan
and China resulted in a resurgence of Japanese interest in
drinking tea. The man largely responsible for this was a

Buddhist monk named Eisai Myo-an. Eisai studied with monks of the southern Zen school in China, learning about matters of spirit—and matters of taste, in the form of tea. Although Eisai is probably best known for introducing Rinzai Zen Buddhism to Japan at the end of the twelfth century, he is also well known (and much appreciated) for bringing the knowledge of whipped, powdered tea from China. The Japanese believed, just as the Chinese did, that the taste of whipped tea was far more pleasing and flavorful than that of tea made from ground tea brick. Tea, prepared in this manner, became enormously popular in Japan.

New converts to Zen Buddhism quickly learned to appreciate tea as well. It was valued initially as an aid to meditation, then later for the taste itself. Eisai was a strong believer in the benefits of drinking tea, and among his prolific writings is the *Kissa Yojoki*, which is variously translated as *Book of Tea Sanitation*, *Drinking Tea for Health*, or *Tea Drinking for the Cultivation of Life*. This work describes tea as a "divine remedy and a supreme gift of heaven" essential for preserving life. Eisai recommends it as a cure for five diseases: loss of appetite, illnesses caused by poor drinking water, paralysis, boils, and beriberi. He concludes with the claim that tea is beneficial for almost all disorders.

"In the great country of China," he states, "they drink tea, as a result of which there is no heart trouble and people live long lives. Our country is full of sickly looking skinny persons, and this is simply because we do not drink tea. When the whole body feels weak, devitalized and

Eisai Myo-an

depressed, it is a sign that the heart is ailing. Drink lots of tea, and one's energy and spirits will be restored to full strength."

The *Kissa Yojoki* goes on to explain not only the effect of tea on each of the human organs but also the psychospiritual results of drinking tea, setting the stage for the formation of the Japanese tea ceremony. Eisai associated drinking tea with elements of Zen, of being fully and completely present, making something as simple as preparing and drinking tea into a spiritual experience.

Eisai's disciple Dogen (1200–1253) is most famous as the patriarch of the Soto sect of Zen Buddhism in Japan, but he also shared his teacher's fervor for tea. He, too, studied in China, and when he returned to Japan in 1227, he brought with him many utensils used for the preparation and serving of tea in China.

During this period, tea was only enjoyed by monks, members of the court, warriors, and high-ranking families. Within the monasteries, taking tea together became an important daily ritual. Tea was served at the first gathering of the monks in the morning. Soon, monks ritualized this gathering by introducing rules for preparing and serving tea, a tradition that eventually became known as *sarei*, the etiquette of making tea. Thus, another step was taken toward the development of the formal tea ceremony, as monks in the twelfth and thirteenth centuries gathered each morning to ceremoniously begin their day with a bowl of whipped green tea.

Although the early years of fourteenth-century Japan were full of political and social upheaval, it was a time of rich cultural expression, and one during which the country continued to develop a national identity. Japanese artists cultivated unique styles in poetry, theater, garden design, ink paintings, and floral designs—and the preparation and serving of tea flourished as well.

The popularity of tea continued to rise during this time for two different reasons. The first was that it was still such an important and valued part of monastery life, and the second was that many more people learned about tea, as it was carried from one place to another by travelers.

From the time that Eisai introduced it as an aid to meditation, tea became an essential part of a monk's life. At this time, tea was grown and processed only at the monasteries,

A page from the twelfth-century
Kissa Yojoki

and the monks were the first tea masters in Japan. As a result, the association between Zen and tea continued to solidify. As more and more people visited the Buddhist temples and Shinto shrines, merchants set up carts and wagons to sell local tea to the travelers. In this way, word of the taste of tea spread quickly throughout the country. When travelers returned to their homes and villages, they spoke of the new beverage from China, and demand for tea began to rise. Tea was soon being grown in places other than the monasteries, and tea gardens were planted in many places throughout Japan. Honyama, in the prefecture of Shizuoka, quickly became the center of the Japanese tea trade, and remains today one of the most important tea-producing regions in Japan.

And so, from its popularity within the religious communities, tea found its way into the hearts, minds, and mouths of people of all classes throughout Japan. The monks took meticulous care in processing and serving the tea, and this same attention to detail quickly came to be important when sharing a bowl of tea, wherever people came together in the countryside or in the villages.

The sharing of tea with friends, even in these early years, was a manifestation of traditional Japanese values, which placed great importance on close family and community ties. Shared tea meant shared friendships as well.

TEA AND THE SAMURAI

The taste for tea continued to spread throughout Japan. The Kamakura era (c. 1192–1333) was called the "Age of Warriors" in Japan, a period when the samurai class ruled. One tale relates that the powerful samurai Minamoto Shogun, born in 1203, became quite ill from overindulging in food and drink, despite his legendary strength and prowess. Learning of Eisai's skill at healing, he summoned him and asked for his help. Eisai offered not only prayers but tea as well, and Minamoto soon recovered. The samurai was, of course, interested in the remedy and obtained a copy of Eisai's book. After reading it, he quickly became an enthusiastic advocate for the use of tea.

The power and influence of the samurai during this period cannot be overstated, and they contributed significantly to the spread of teahouses, the tea ceremony, and the

general popularity of the beverage. When entering a tea-house, the warriors literally put down their swords, leaving them outside as they enjoyed the cultural and peaceful experience of sharing tea.

According to one description of *bushido*, or "the way of the warrior," the samurai code of honor, "A samurai whose only attribute is strength is not acceptable. He must use his leisure time to practice poetry and understand the tea ceremony." The experience of serving tea in a precise way took the warrior out of his everyday existence, which placed such emphasis on strength and endurance, and offered him an opportunity for enriching his soul as well.

TOCHA—TEA GAMES AND GATHERINGS

Although there were still mystical and spiritual aspects of serving and sharing tea during the mid-fourteenth century in Japan, by this point in history, teahouses had become quite secular and boisterous. The sharing of tea, begun by the Buddhist monks, had lost much of its Zenlike quality.

Outside the monasteries, tea gatherings became more and more festive, and eventually games and contests were included in these assemblies. A popular game was one in which individuals guessed the origin of different teas being served. A true tea connoisseur could guess not only the region from which the tea came, but even the actual farm or garden where it was grown. Tea games and contests were called *tocha*. Prizes for winning competitions included items such as silk, armor, and jewelry. Tocha was also known as *juppuku-cha*, meaning "ten cups of tea," or *gojup-puku-cha*, "fifty cups of tea," referring to the many cups of tea drunk by participants.

There are many myths and legends about the excesses of the tea gatherings of this day. Some stories say that up to one hundred cups per person were served at events that sometimes lasted from morning well into the night. Probably only one actual cup or bowl was used, and this was passed from one person to the next. Many of these gatherings included not only the serving of tea, but also alcohol; they could be wild and rowdy affairs, with gambling, poetry reading, music, and even bathing.

One of the more colorful figures of the time was Sasaki Doyo (1295–1373), a *daimyo* (literally, "great name"), a powerful feudal ruler. Sasaki led a rich and ostentatious lifestyle that included frequent tocha gatherings, and he became famous for them. He even developed an incense contest, similar to tocha, called *toko*, in which participants tried to guess the origin of hundreds of different incense fragrances.

Tocha often took place in a room called a *kissa-no-tei*, usually an upstairs room of an establishment. The host was called *teishu*, a term still used today to refer to the host of a tea gathering or tea ceremony.

The Ashikaga shoguns, who ruled between 1336 and 1572, practiced *shoin*, an elaborate and ostentatious serving of tea, done with great ceremony and deliberation in vast halls. The utensils developed to prepare and serve tea at shoin became almost as important as the tea itself.

The cultural aspects of these elaborate parties, all of which revolved around the serving of tea, were explored in Herbert Plutschow's essay "An Anthropological Perspective on the Japanese Tea Ceremony" (1999). Plutschow suggests that political and military leaders used these elaborate tea ceremonies not only to impress people with their wealth and power, but also as a "reaffirmation of social and political order." Guests, for example, were seated according to a strict hierarchy and served tea in order of their rank.

During this time, serving tea became a political tool. Depending on how the ceremony was presented—where the guests were seated and the type and number of utensils involved—the tea ceremony was used to unify rank, impress visitors, or promote peace and friendship. No matter how it was used, however, the idea of the tea ceremony became the antithesis of war and brutality. The teahouse was the polar opposite of the battlefield.

When civil war came to an end at the close of the fourteenth century, tocha was officially banned because the ruling powers believed that the large, raucous gatherings contributed to rioting and unrest. But tocha was such a part of everyday life that the ban was generally ignored. Commoners and soldiers still enjoyed boisterous tea games, while samurai nobles and aristocrats continued to experience slightly more sophisticated, but still ostentatious, tea gatherings.

AGE OF THE JAPANESE TEA MASTERS

Early Masters: Ikkyu, Shuko, and Takeno Joo

Prince Ikkyu, who lived at the beginning of the fifteenth century (1394–1481), was one of first people to try to lure the warriors and aristocrats away from the excesses of tea, and to begin to restore the tea ceremony to its simpler, more meditative style. This prince became a priest at age eleven and enjoyed a full and exciting life. Apparently, Ikkyu was both quick-witted and full of humor, showing a great zest for life. One of the best-loved stories about Ikkyu relates

that when he was still a young monk, one of his duties was to bring his master tea in his favorite bowl. One day, Ikkyu tripped as he carried the tea, and the master's favorite bowl shattered into a thousand pieces. Quickly, Ikkyu swept up the shards and, hiding them in his robes, went to see the master. "Master, why do people die?" he asked.

The master answered, "It is natural. Everything in the world has a life and a death."

"Everything?" Ikkyu asked.

"Everything," the master answered firmly.

At this point, Ikkyu showed his master the shattered pieces of the tea bowl and said, "It seems that your tea bowl has experienced an untimely death."

Ikkyu's longest-reaching contribution to our use of tea, however, was as a teacher, for his most famous student was Murata Shuko, who created what would become the famous Japanese tea ceremony.

Shuko (1423–1502) was born in Nara, and, during his youth, was undoubtedly exposed to the tea games and ceremonies so popular at the time. However, the rowdy, secular gatherings would not have appealed to Shuko, whose nature was more sedate and spiritual.

Shuko chose to enter the Buddhist priesthood and was under the tutelage of Ikkyu from 1474 until his teacher's death in 1481. Ikkyu, who knew both Chinese and Korean ways of serving tea, shared this knowledge with his disciple. The influence of his teacher and his training in Zen meditation convinced Shuko that the tea ceremony could be much more than entertainment. He believed that it could serve as a means to deep meditation and even a path to enlightenment, in accordance with the Zen teaching that every daily act, no matter how mundane, can lead to enlightenment, if performed in the right spirit.

Shuko, who was also a skilled architect, believed that participating in the tea ceremony could bring greater enlightenment than hours of meditation, but that the room in which this was done had to be conducive to the experience. Traditionally, the size of a Japanese room was designated by the number of tatami mats (woven straw mats) that would fit in it. Each mat measured 90 by 180 by 5 centimeters (35 by 70 by 2 inches). A half-mat measured 90 by 90 by 5 centimeters (35 by 35 by 2 inches).

Shuko designed a tea hut that was a "four and a half mat" space in the city of Kyoto, creating an area that was differentiated from its surroundings both physically and philosophically.

This small room was in sharp contrast to the huge banquet halls used by the ruling class of the time, and it illustrated the simple nature of the ceremony Shuko promoted. Vimalakirti may have entertained 84,000 heavenly beings in a small room, according to Buddhist legend, but mere mortals take up more space. There was simply not enough room in such a small space to make much of a political statement, and the close quarters contributed to a feeling of equality.

Shuko believed that creating a special space for tea, even in the city, offered a place for enjoyment of the noble arts, and that the tea hut itself could be symbolic. The tea hut was reserved for the express purpose of the ritualistic serving of tea, and was not used for everyday activities. The threshold of the tea hut became a symbolic boundary which, when crossed, allowed people to enter into a different realm and participate in something sacred and ritualistic, juxtaposed with their normal, everyday lives. Thus, the space lent itself to a deeper connection between the human and the divine.

According to Herbert Plutschow, author of "An Anthropological Perspective on the Tea Ceremony," the tearoom becomes "a world unto itself, where continuity of ordinary space and time, dependent on our physical existence, ceases to exist. Within such a room, one is a disembodied spirit, unencumbered by material limitations. In such a room, there is no absolute time, only the ever changing 'now.'"

The idea of serving tea in places separate from ordinary living space was readily accepted by those tired of the ostentation of the great tea debaucheries. Small, humble teahouses, called *soan cha*, were actually simple, thatched-roofed huts. As these small structures gained in popularity, features were added that helped practitioners feel a greater separation from their everyday lives when they sat and shared tea.

Shuko's idea was to simplify the tea ceremony in all ways. He was also one of the first to encourage the use of Japanese utensils and ware, instead of Chinese. Trade between Japan and China had reopened in 1401, and Japan was again much enamored with all things Chinese during the fifteenth century. The tea ceremony was an opportunity to show off beautiful and expensive Chinese ware to one's friends. While Shuko did not dismiss the beauty found in implements and utensils made in China, he did suggest the advantages of using wares created in Japan. In a letter to one of his disciples, Shuko advocated an equality between the Chinese and Japanese cultures, writing that it was good to find worthwhile and admirable traits in Japanese things as well as those from China.

Shuko's disciple was Takeno Joo (1504–1555), the son of a wealthy merchant who lived in the port city of Sakai. He was interested in many of the arts, and in Sakai he was able to see firsthand many of the imports from China, including the newest tea utensils. By the end of his life, he had accumulated an unprecedented sixty different kinds of tea utensils, while most tea masters only had three or four. In spite of his love of refined art, he believed in the teachings of Shuko, who advocated simplicity, particularly in terms of sharing tea. He even simplified Shuko's four-and-a-half-mat tea hut, replacing the paper walls with earthen ones, and using bamboo lattice in place of the fine woods. He preferred the most simple setting possible and the most straightforward utensils. His tearoom was large enough for just five people.

Rulers and Nobles: Nobunaga and Hideyoshi

Portuguese traders first came to Japan in 1549, bringing with them the religion of Christianity and opening up new markets. One of the results of this was a new middle class of merchants, who quickly became powerful in their own right. During the sixteenth century, the city of Sakai was the most active commercial center in Japan and home to a thriving middle class. As a result, the city was ruled more democratically than others in Japan, and the administration of the city was run by merchants and businessmen. Of course, these men took care not to insult or in any way disturb the powerful lords and warriors, and they made efforts to establish and maintain friendly ties with them. The tea ceremony presented the perfect opportunity for doing this, since one of the essential elements of the ceremony was equality. Tea gatherings were generally small affairs, held in private homes.

In addition to these small at-home affairs, government

"Tea should be taken in solitude."
—*C. S. Lewis (1898–1963)*

leaders also reinstated the use of the tea ceremony for political purposes, as had been done in the fourteenth century. One of the best examples of this practice is Oda Nobunaga (1534–1582), who was one of Japan's most powerful rulers. He used the opportunities presented by the tea ceremony, just as government officials today use a state banquet, as a means of solidifying friendships with wealthy merchants and engendering political favors. Indeed, he was so famous for his use of the tea ceremony that his government was sometimes called the *ochanoyu goseido* or the *cha-no-yu* (the "hot water for tea" or "tea ceremony") government.

Nobunaga was well versed in the way of tea, and letters and papers written during his rule tell us that he often served tea himself. Because the tea ceremony was such an important political tool, however, it was customary for rulers to enlist the help of a tea master. His choice for official government tea master was Sen Rikyu, considered the "father of the modern tea ceremony."

After Nobunaga's death, his successor, Toyotomi Hideyoshi (1536–1598), also chose Rikyu to serve as tea master, a position that held great power and prestige. Hideyoshi continued the governmental use of the tea ceremony to secure political allies. These tea events were large affairs, to which all the important families and wealthy merchants were invited.

Hideyoshi loved the grand exuberance of a large tea gathering. At his opulent and beautiful castle in Osaka, he built a "golden tea room," a portable room that was actually taken to Kyoto for a special tea ceremony honoring the Emperor Ogimachi, a gathering for which Rikyu served as tea master, consequently gaining much attention and further power.

In addition to the large and ornate, Hideyoshi also appreciated the small, simple tea ceremonies, for which he had a two-mat hut built that he called "Mountain Village," *Yamazato*, where he led the tea ceremony himself.

During the late sixteenth century, many of the samurai joined Hideyoshi in the practice of serving tea in modest, ritualistic spaces, and the philosophy of *wabi* became popular. Wabi is the Japanese art of finding beauty in imperfection and discovering a sense of the profound in all things in nature. The word "wabi" comes from the root word *wa*, which refers to harmony, peace, tranquility, and balance. This concept became quite important in its influence on Japanese culture and on the development of the tea ceremony.

One of the phrases often used to describe wabi is "the joy of the little monk in his wind-torn robe." Those who embraced the idea of wabi participated in the tea ceremony in a simple room, with primitive utensils, in a way that allowed attention to each moment of the ceremony.

The tea master of this time, Sen Rikyu, embraced the idea of wabi and based his tea gatherings on this philosophy. It was his genius that finally molded the serving of the tea into a ceremony so steeped in ritual and so important symbolically that it is still being practiced today in essentially the same way. Rikyu had unparalleled influence on tea and the development of the tea ceremony.

SEN RIKYU AND THE SEVEN RULES OF TEA

Sen Rikyu was by far the most famous of all Japanese tea masters. He was born in 1522 in Sakai and became a pupil of Takeno Joo. Even more than his master, however, Rikyu believed in the spiritual aspects of tea and was a strict adherent of the practice of wabi.

Like his predecessor Shuko, Rikyu preferred utensils and bowls made in Japan to those from China or Korea. His own preference was for dark, somber gray and black ceramics and rough raku bowls (described in Chapter 6). Under his influence, the ceramics industry in Japan changed and grew dramatically. In all things associated with the tea ceremony, Rikyu strove for artistic simplicity. Rather than place elaborate vases and pieces of art in the tearoom, Rikyu chose to use simple artifacts found in almost any home and to arrange them artistically.

Rikyu's seven rules of tea, written in the sixteenth century, explain his attitude toward tea. These rules are: "Make a delicious bowl of tea. Lay out the wood charcoal to heat the water. Arrange the flowers as they are in the fields. In summer, evoke coolness; in winter, warmth. Anticipate the time for everything. Be prepared for rain. Show the greatest attention to each of your guests."

Rikyu showed true genius in regard to the tea ceremony and believed strongly in the spiritual depth that it could reflect. He proposed that the practice of tea, in accordance with Zen principles, should be an egalitarian approach in which class, rank, and religion held no importance. He designed his tea huts so that everyone who entered had to stoop, symbolizing that all people are equal, in spite of rank and class. His teahouses were also designed to heighten an awareness of nature, and even the tea huts in the city gave the appearance of being in a remote, rural locale.

The tea ceremony was an integral part of all Japanese life during the sixteenth century, for tea drinking had spread to commoners as well, by this time. Tea sellers on the streets of Kyoto sold a bowl of low-grade tea for a sen— the coin of least value of the time.

Rikyu served Hideyoshi for many years and became a trusted and intimate companion, who was asked to take charge of the day-to-day working of Hideyoshi's household. He was often asked to perform the tea ceremony and enjoyed a great reputation both at court and among commoners.

But in spite of his affinity for simplicity within the tearoom, Rikyu had an arrogant nature that often irritated Hideyoshi. Even though the men initially enjoyed a close relationship, tensions built over the years until finally Rikyu was ordered by Hideyoshi to commit ritual suicide.

There are many stories explaining the possible reasons for this harsh command. Some accounts say that Hideyoshi demanded that Rikyu's daughter be given to a warlord as a concubine, and Rikyu refused. Another story says that Hideyoshi was jealous of Rikyu because he had such a large and devoted following. Whatever the reason, in 1591, at the age of seventy, Rikyu performed one last tea ceremony, then committed *seppuku*.

The tea ceremony that had developed in Japan by the end of the sixteenth century was the result of the passions and teachings of many men, from Eisai, who brought the first seeds from China and established a new way of preparing and serving tea, to Rikyu, who taught that the tea ceremony offered a place and time to leave worldly concerns behind and to enter for a short time into the realm of the spiritual. The tea masters left a rich legacy in the form of the tea ceremony, a deeply spiritual and symbolic ritual that is still practiced today.

CHAPTER 5

The Japanese Tea Ceremony

"Tea with us became more than an idealization of the
form of drinking; it is a religion of the art of life."

—*Kakuzo Okakura*

IN JAPAN, THE TEA CEREMONY is called *cha-no-yu*, which
translates literally as "water for tea." This, in a nutshell, is
what the tea ceremony is all about. In spite of the rich symbolism, the attention to detail, and the ritualistic acts, the
essence of the tea ceremony remains nothing more than
adding water to tea leaves and then serving it to guests. The
magic is in the manner in which that is done.

Various tea masters through the centuries emphasized
different aspects of the ceremony. Shuko, for example,
taught that the most important element of the tea ceremony was the right attitude. Purity of mind, he said, is
more important even than cleanliness. He went on to say
that treating all guests with equality, self-control, and consideration was more important than honoring distin-
guished guests.

Takeno Joo, who followed in his master's footsteps, suggested that a tea master must essentially practice what he
preaches. Thus, one's ability to perform the tea ceremony
with purity of mind was enhanced if he could perform all
acts of life from this viewpoint, treating all with whom he
came in contact with reverence and honor.

Up until the time of Rikyu's ritual suicide, knowledge of the rules and etiquette of the tea ceremony was passed on from a tea master to his students. Rikyu's grandson, Sen Sotan (1578–1658), formalized his grandfather's teachings to be used in a school dedicated to *chado* ("the way of tea"), also known as *sado*. Cha-no-yu refers to a single ceremony, but chado is the study of the doctrine of the tea ceremony.

Sen Sotan divided his property into three parts, and at his death, each of his three sons inherited a piece of land. Each developed a different tea school: Urasenke, Omotesenke, and Mushanokoji. Today, Mushanokoji and Omotesenke are relatively unknown outside Japan. Both use the word sado to describe their study of tea. Urasenke is the school best known outside Japan, and they use the term chado.

TEA, SPIRIT, AND SYMBOLISM

Of course, the tea ceremony is much more than simply the preparation and serving of a cup of tea. In *The Book of Tea*, Kakuzo Okakura wrote, "Tea with us became more than an idealization of the form of drinking; it is a religion of the art of life."

There is a deep and important association between Zen and the tea ceremony that developed over several hundred years. "Zen and tea are one and the same" is a saying that has been repeated countless times, with good reason. From the very beginning, it was the Zen Buddhist priests who took an interest in tea, for they believed that drinking it would help keep them awake and alert for the long periods of meditation that their religion required.

As the tea ceremony developed, particularly during the sixteenth century, many Zenlike ideas were embraced within this ritual. The elements of simplicity and purity, important in Zen Buddhism, also greatly influenced the development of the cha-no-yu. The practice of Zen and the tea ceremony shared many of the same qualities, each creating a sense of peace and well-being and a diminishing of the ego, bringing one closer to an awareness of the divine. Daisetz T. Suzuki (1870–1966), author of many books on Buddhism and Zen, said, "If you understand one thing completely, you understand all things," and it is this idea, perhaps, that underlies the importance of the tea ceremony.

There are, however, important differences between Zen and the tea ceremony. Zen is a path to enlightenment. The tea ceremony is an opportunity for individuals to share a spiritual experience, though not a religious one. In tea, there is no god or divinity.

One of the greatest gifts that cha-no-yu offers is an environment, separate from the everyday pace and place, where the participants can commune with their host and other guests, but also begin to look at ordinary items with fresh eyes, finding beauty in the mundane.

The tea ceremony also provides an opportunity to practice being in accord with nature and to feel a harmony with the seasons. A love of nature, the ancients believed, is the basis for awakening an appreciation of beauty and, therefore, of art. The classic tearoom or hut was built to blend in with its surroundings. The walls of the hut were made of logs with the bark still attached, or were sometimes simply plastered with mud. The house was situated to display to best advantage the changing of the seasons and of the sunlight and shadow during the day. Each ceremony performed there was in accord with the season of the year. Flowers used in the arrangements were those that grew or bloomed naturally during that time. The food offered was also seasonal.

No matter when or where the ceremony takes place, however, it is built on the concept of *ichigo ichie* ("one time, one meeting"), a phrase that means that every encounter is unique and never repeats in a lifetime. One lives this particular moment, and then it is gone. The emphasis is on being aware of each moment, in a ritualized way.

PREPARING FOR THE CEREMONY

The etiquette of the tea ceremony is full of ritual and symbolism. Though it may seem meaningless to the uninitiated, to those who have studied the art of tea, each movement holds a special significance. Each ceremony is imbued with the principles set forth by Rikyu: harmony, respect, purity, and tranquility.

There are three basic elements to the ceremony, each one of which holds equal importance. These include:

1. The arrangement of the utensils, host, guests, food and drink, and each item in the teahouse. Every element should

be placed so that the tea master can reach it with easy, smooth movements.

2. The purification and cleanliness of each item used in the ceremony. Each item used, including the tea caddy, scoop, bowls, whisk, and the rest, is ceremoniously wiped clean, symbolizing the spiritual cleansing of the heart and mind.

3. The calmness of mind of each of the participants, including host and guests.

THE CEREMONY

Traditionally, the host (teishu) wore a kimono, but today sometimes formal Western-style clothing is worn. The guests, too, wear formal clothing of quiet or somber colors. The host greets the guests, bows, and leads them through the low door of the teahouse. Guests are seated first, then the host sits.

The meal is served first, and varies according to the season and the type of ceremony being performed. After the guests have eaten, the host may invite them to retire to the garden while he (or she) prepares the tea. Once all is ready, the host summons the guests by means of a gong (during the day) or a bell (in the evening).

All the utensils used for the ceremony are precisely laid out. The host first uses the *fukusa* (silk cloth) to purify the tea caddy and the scoop. This cloth is thought to represent the spirit of the host, and it is handled with great concentration and reverence. The host then ladles a bit of hot water into the tea bowl, rinses the whisk in this, then pours out the water and wipes the utensils dry with a white cloth called the *chakin*.

The host then scoops the tea into the tea bowl, ladles hot water into the bowl, and whisks it. The bowl is offered first to the principal guest, who holds it and turns it around to admire it before tasting the tea. After tasting it, he or she wipes the rim of the bowl and passes it on to the next guest, and so on.

After all the guests have taken tea, the remainder of the tea is discarded, and the bowl is rinsed and dried, as are the scoop and the whisk. The tea master should not only collect and use the utensils, but also have an appreciation of them. To use them without knowing their value is not considered to be in the true spirit of cha-no-yu.

After the ceremony, the various utensils should be offered to the guests for their inspection. According to

etiquette, guests should ask about each of them. If no one asks questions about them, the host takes it as a sign that the utensils are simply not interesting enough to stimulate conversation and discussion. It is thus the responsibility of the guests to show interest in each item, so as not to offend the host.

After the guests admire the various utensils, they prepare to leave the world of tea, both physically and symbolically.

ESSENTIALS OF THE TEA CEREMONY

The Tea

Today, just as it was in the days of Rikyu, powdered green tea, known as matcha, is used. This can be either *koicha*, thick tea, or *usucha*, thin tea. Traditionally, koicha was made from the buds of aged tea plants, usually between thirty and eighty years old. A thick, pasty tea was made, using a large quantity of tea powder, usually about six teaspoons per three-fourths cup of water. Because the tea is so thick, when water is added to the bowl, it is stirred slowly to make a paste. This has a sweetish, mellow taste.

Usucha uses only half to one-third the amount of tea needed for koicha, usually two to three teaspoons per three-fourths cup of water. Hot water is added to the bowl, and the whisk is moved back and forth quickly until foam appears. This makes the famous "whipped green tea," known as "frothy jade" since the time of the Song dynasty.

Utensils

The utensils for the ceremony, called *dogu* (literally, "tools"), are chosen carefully. Some are simply for show, others are actually used in the serving of the tea, but each is selected for its inherent value—based either on its beauty or its usefulness.

Though there is some variation in the number and type of utensils used for different ceremonies, the following utensils are generally considered important ones:

Chashaku. The spoon or ladle used for scooping the tea into the bowl. These were originally made from ivory or metal, but many tea masters did not like to use metals, and bamboo eventually became the material of choice. Many tea masters carved their own spoons, decorating them with various designs.

Chakin. A rectangular cloth, usually made of white linen or hemp, used for cleaning the tea bowl.

Fukusa. A square cloth, usually made of plain colored silk (usually purple for men and orange or red for women), used to clean the scoop and tea caddy. The host keeps the fukusa tucked into the obi of a kimono while he or she is not using it.

Chasen. The whisk used for stirring or "whipping" the powdered tea after water is added. This is usually made out of a single piece of bamboo, split into tiny pieces and tied with thread. Each thin strip is curled around to make a loop. Two different kinds of whisks are used, depending on the type of tea served. The *kuzuho* is thin and sparse at the head and is used for whipping thin tea. The *araho* is thick and dense and is used for thick tea.

When the whisk has lost its shape and is no longer useful, it is not thrown away but kept until spring, usually until May, when it is ceremoniously burned in a ritual called *chasen koyo*. This is in keeping with the respect shown for all elements of the tea ceremony.

Natsume. A laquered tea caddy used to hold usucha, thin tea. It is named for its shape, which is similar to that of the *natsume*, or jujube fruit. Generally, it has a rounded bottom, is wide and thick, and has a flat top. The *cha-ire* is used to hold tea for making koicha, thick tea. It is traditionally ceramic, and is long and narrow with a more elaborate top or lid, often made with ivory and gold.

Chawan. This is the tea bowl, perhaps the most important element used in the tea ceremony. These vary tremendously in size, shape, sophistication, and beauty. Different bowls are used for thin and thick teas, for formal and casual ceremonies, and for different seasons of the year. During summer, for example, shallow bowls are used, to allow the tea to cool rapidly. In winter, the bowls are more narrow and deep, allowing the tea to remain hot longer.

Even today, when bowls break—which they inevitably do—they are sometimes painstakingly repaired instead of being thrown away. Traditionally, the mended bowls are used in ceremonies late in the year (November and December), when the concepts of simplicity and humbleness (wabi) are emphasized.

Chashitsu, the Tearoom

According to the strictest principles of Zen, not even the tearoom itself should be permanent, as only the soul is eternal.

Of course, there were, and still are, rooms and small houses that are set aside for the sole purpose of cha-no-yu. In these, the room remains empty except for the implements and decorations brought in for each individual ceremony. The tea master chooses embellishments carefully and avoids repetition. For example, if a flower arrangement is used, a scroll depicting calligraphy, rather than flowers, is hung. If the tea caddy is long and narrow, then the tea kettle is round, and so on.

Traditionally, the tearoom is just large enough to hold four and a half tatami mats, and placement is important for determining how people walk through the room. Usually, there is a center mat, on which the tea utensils are placed for viewing, and the other mats are placed around this.

According to tradition, people should shuffle, rather than stride, when walking on tatamis. This helps one maintain correct posture, slow down, and to walk quietly, all characteristics in keeping with the philosophy of the tea ceremony.

Decoration

The flower arrangements used in the teahouse are called *chabana*. They differ from *ikebana*, Japanese floral arrangements used throughout the house. The host arranges the flowers in the most natural way, simply putting them in a vase. Brightly colored flowers are avoided, and white flowers are not used while there is still snow on the ground.

Very few flowers are used in chabana, usually only one large flower in the center with a smaller flower or bud on the side. Too many leaves or flowers take away from the simple beauty.

A hanging scroll, called a *kakemono*, is almost always placed in the tearoom. These are usually brush paintings of nature—birds, trees, flowers, or landscapes—or calligraphy of poems, Buddhist sayings, or teachings of some of the famous masters. One of the favorite themes for calligraphy scrolls is Rikyu's principles of the tea ceremony: harmony, respect, purity, and tranquility.

"I always fear that creation will expire before teatime."
—*Sydney Smith (1771–1845), English writer and clergyman*

TEA GARDENS

The tea garden is created for viewing from the teahouse. During the Muromachi period in Japan (1333–1573), after a large banquet, guests went to the garden to rest in cool air before they went on to the pavilion to have tea.

Although each garden is unique, the following are common elements:

Plants. All plants are used symbolically, and few flowering plants are used, as they are considered too distracting. For example, trees, usually evergreens such as pine and cedar or deciduous trees such as oak, are planted to look like remote mountains. Moss is used in abundance to remind viewers of mountain scenery.

Wash basin. A stone basin (*tsukubai*) is placed outside the tearoom. Originally, guests used this water to rinse their mouths and wash their hands before the tea ceremony. Now

"In my own hands I hold a bowl of tea; I see all of nature represented in its green color. Closing my eyes I find green mountains and pure water within my own heart. Silently sitting alone and drinking tea, I feel these become a part of me."

—*Soshitsu Sen, Grand Master XIV, Urasenke School of Tea*

"The most trying hours in life are between four o'clock and the evening meal. A cup of tea at this time adds a lot of comfort and happiness."

—*Royal S. Copeland, M.D.,*
former health commissioner
of New York City, Dec. 1925

the washing is done more for the symbolism than the cleanliness, but it remains an important act of purifying before beginning the ceremony. The word *tsukubai*, which means "crouching," was used because the basin is small and low to the ground.

Stone lantern (*ishi-doro*). Stone lanterns were introduced to Japan from China and Korea through Buddhist priests, for they were originally used in temples, and then later in Shinto shrines. A large lantern is placed beside the wash basin, and other smaller lanterns are placed throughout the garden.

Bench. A bench where the guests wait, called *koshikake machiai*. It is sometimes protected by a wooden arbor. This is a place for guests to sit quietly before entering the tea room.

Garden path. The garden path, or *roji* (which literally means "earth damp with dew"), is a stone path connecting the bench with the tearoom. The stones vary in size, depending on the scale of the garden, but they are almost always surrounded with moss and small, low-growing plants. Walking along the roji allows guests to enter the first stage of the meditation of the tea ceremony. This is considered a passage into a more inward place and is intended to help prepare the guest for the experience of the tearoom. Kakuzo Okakura, author of *The Book of Tea*, wrote, "One who has trodden this garden path cannot fail to remember how his spirit . . . became uplifted above ordinary thoughts."

Rikyu, the sixteenth-century tea master, thought the secret of a successful tea garden was found in this ancient, anonymous poem:

> *I looked beyond;*
> *Flowers are not,*
> *Nor tinted leaves.*
> *On the sea beach*
> *A solitary cottage stands*
> *In the waning light*
> *Of an autumn eve.*

CHAPTER 6

Tea in the Ming Dynasty

"Tea is drunk to forget the din of the world."

—*Tien Yiheng, Chinese poet*

THE FIRST STEEPED TEA

During the rule of the Mongols in China (early 1200s through 1368), tea lost much of its popularity and, for a while, was considered just another beverage. During the Ming dynasty (1368–1644), however, new and innovative methods of processing the leaves caused a renewal of interest in tea, and it regained its popularity throughout the country. Instead of being beaten into a powder that was then whipped, the leaves were picked, withered, rolled, dried, and oxidized. The new process created a product composed of dried, loose tea leaves, which, when steeped in hot or boiling water, yielded a delicious, full-bodied, and smooth-tasting beverage—the same that we enjoy today. There are exceptions, of course—Tibetans still use brick tea, and the Japanese still use powdered tea (matcha) in the tea ceremony—but this was the final step in the evolution of tea processing.

Loose tea, steeped to make the beverage, was used throughout China. Testimony to the popularity of steeped tea comes from Emperor Hong-wu, the first ruler of the Ming dynasty, who required that the imperial tribute tea be sent as loose tea, rather than in bricks, as had previously been required. Not only did this tea taste better, it also was easier to process. The leaves were pan-fried, rather than steamed, which saved much time. (This is still done in China; in Japan, tea leaves are still steamed.)

Along with an enhanced taste, the loose-leaf process developed during the Ming dynasty allowed for the addition of many different items (usually spices or fruits, or teas from different regions) to create tea blends. The Ming dynasty's obsession with flowers manifested itself not only in poetry and art, but in tea as well—it was during this period that various flowers were used to flavor tea. Although tea masters used many different flowers, including rose, magnolia, osmanthus, and lichee, by far the most popular was (and still is) jasmine. These additives further enhanced the sweetness of the beverage and helped fuel an avid love of tea in Ming China. People of the Ming dynasty drank tea for solace, for celebration, and for any number of other reasons, as evidenced by the following entry from a Ming dynasty tea manual:

> *Times for drinking tea:*
> *In idle moments*
> *When bored with poetry*
> *Thoughts confused*
> *Beating time to songs*
> *When music stops*
> *Living in seclusion*
> *Enjoying scholarly pastimes*
> *Conversing late at night*

Studying on a sunny day
In the bridal chamber
Detaining favoured guests
Playing host to scholars or pretty girls
Visiting friends returned from far away
In perfect weather
When skies are overcast
Watching boats glide past on the canal
Midst trees and bamboos
When flowers bud and birds chatter
On hot days by a lotus pond
Burning incense in the courtyard
After tipsy guests have left
When the youngsters have gone out
On visits to secluded temples
When viewing springs and scenic rocks.

—Hsu Tze-shu, *Ch'a Shu*

NEW VESSELS FOR BREWING TEA

The new method of brewing tea required different utensils and, particularly, different vessels for holding the beverage. When tea was made by boiling leaves shaved from a hard tea brick, it was brewed in open pans over a fire. When it came in a powder form, a wide-mouthed bowl was needed for whisking. When loose tea leaves were steeped in hot water for several minutes, it was found that small, covered containers brought out the fullest flavors, and the idea of a teapot was born.

There is much controversy about who actually invented the first "tea pot." The answer depends on how you define a teapot. When the Chinese made the switch to brewed tea, they probably used a vessel they were already familiar with, and which was available to them, a wine ewer. Wine ewers, small containers used to hold warm wine, had been used since the Song dynasty. These vessels were round or slightly oval and had a curved spout and a top handle. Since they were suitable for holding hot liquids, ewers made excellent vessels for brewed tea.

As these ewers were used more frequently for tea and less for wine, the design was altered to better accommodate the brewing of tea. Although a top handle made it easy to carry hot wine, it became cumbersome when the ewer was used for tea. The handle got in the way when it came time to clean out the residue, after the leaves had been steeped. The solution was to put the handle on the side of the pot, rather than the top. When Europeans first began importing tea and tea ware during the centuries to come, it was these ewers rather than actual teapots that were shipped from China westward. Queen Mary had a Chinese wine ewer in her collection in the mid-sixteenth century.

When large containers were used for brewing tea in great quantities, the tea often became bitter because it was not consumed immediately. Then as now, the longer tea brews, the worse it tastes, as more chemicals called tannins are released from the leaves. Tannins contribute to the taste and pungency of tea, but if too much is released into the brew, it turns bitter and astringent—as all who have overbrewed a cup of tea can attest. The Chinese of the Ming dynasty realized that it made sense to brew up smaller

The History of Processing Tea—in a Nutshell

The most ancient way to prepare tea was to take the raw leaves off the shrub and drop them into boiling water. The result was a bitter, unpleasant liquid, primarily used as medicine.

The taste of tea improved somewhat when the leaves were dried and pressed into a brick. Bits and pieces were cut off the brick and boiled in water, creating a beverage that was still coarse and acidic.

The next improvement occurred when the leaves were steamed, dried, and ground into a fine powder. The tea drinker put a spoonful of the powder in a wide-mouthed bowl, added hot water, and stirred it with a bamboo whisk. The taste of whipped tea was decidedly better, offering a fresh, grassy flavor.

The final step in the evolution of tea processing occurred when the leaves were steamed, cut, oxidized (allowed to ferment for a period of hours), dried, and sorted. The resulting product was steeped in hot or boiling water for several minutes and then strained and enjoyed. The taste of tea had finally come of age.

(For a full explanation of tea-processing methods, see Chapter 1.)

---

quantities and to fix a fresh pot when more was needed. So, along with altering the placement of the handle, they reduced the size of the vessel. They even made miniature pots and used them to brew the highest-quality (and correspondingly, the most expensive) teas, which were sipped and savored slowly.

MING PORCELAIN AND POTTERY

The revival of tea's popularity corresponded to an increased interest in porcelain and pottery. Porcelain had been produced in China since the time of the T'ang dynasty (618–907). It was made from kaolin (china clay) and feldspar (china stone) and was fired at a very high temperature to make a hard, translucent, white material. The Chinese

Japan in Isolation—
Seventeenth and Early Eighteenth Centuries

Japan, under Shogun rule, became increasingly isolated during the first part of the seventeenth century. By 1630, the British had abandoned their trading post at Hirado, and with it, attempts at trading with the Japanese. By the middle of the century, all foreigners had been asked to leave, and no foreign trade was permitted. Japan, isolated from the West, continued to develop a culture as sophisticated as any in the world.

This period of polished civilization was not to last, however, for during the eighteenth century, famine and civil unrest brought great difficulties to Japan. In spite of repeated efforts by the Russians, Dutch, and English, Japan remained closed to foreigners until 1854, when Commodore Perry arrived and negotiated with Japan to open trade relations with the United States, resulting in the Treaty of Kanagawa. This was quickly followed by treaties with Great Britain, Russia, and Holland.

ranked the quality of porcelain not only by how it looked or the color and beauty of the glaze, but also by the sound it made when struck. Thick pottery, when struck lightly, produced a dull thud. Fine porcelain, which is harder and more closely compacted, made a more musical, metallic sound.

Light-colored ceramics, which showed off the colors of the brewed tea, became fashionable during the Ming dynasty, particularly white or off-white tea ware, which became all the rage. The most popular was porcelain painted with an underglaze of cobalt blue. "Blue and white" ware was considered the finest available.

The Ming dynasty was characterized by a passionate love of nature, which translated into naturalistic motifs painted

點 提 湯

A Chinese tea pot
(as depicted in the *Ch'a Ching*, 780 CE)

on the clay, particularly on that used for serving and drinking tea. Popular pottery decoration of the times included the lotus, tree branches, and animals. The best pots were named and signed by the artist, and the tea ware of the greatest artists was eagerly bought by Chinese royalty and intellectuals.

Yixing Pots

The three main centers for making tea ware in China during the Ming dynasty were Dehua, Jingdezhen, and Yixing. The most popular and still the most famous of all teapots were made from a clay that the Chinese call *zisha*, a purple clay that was found in the area around Yixing, located about 120 miles northwest of Shanghai.

Clay from the Yixing region had been used to make pots since the Song dynasty, but it was only in the Ming period, when the teapot came into favor, that these pots attained their greatest fame.

Though called "purple," the clay occurred naturally in three different colors—light cream, red, and a purplish brown; the higher the concentration of iron, the deeper the color. Other colors and shades were created by mixing these three colors of clay or adding other pigments such as cobalt oxide or magnesium oxide.

Potters dug the clay, dried it, pounded it into a powder, and passed it through a bamboo sieve to remove pebbles and stones. The sifted powder was then placed in a 1.5-meter (five feet) deep pool filled with fresh water. After three days, the mud was removed and dried in the sun, then cut into blocks. Artists then pounded the blocks with wooden mallets and added more water to make a moldable clay from which the pots were formed.

The pots made from this clay remained porous and absorbed the flavor and fragrance of the tea, so that the vessel itself actually contributed to the taste of a cup of tea. So much of the essence was absorbed by the pots that it became customary to use only one type of tea with a particular pot, so as not to mix and confuse the flavors. Tea connoisseurs of the Ming period claimed that if one used the same pot daily, and used it for only one type of tea, that after many years, the pot would have absorbed so much flavor that one wouldn't even need to add tea anymore—just hot water!

A popular myth tells about a nobleman who loved both tea and the vessels in which it was brewed. He spent much of his time and fortune collecting the finest tea ware and tea leaves available. One day a beggar arrived at his doorstep and said to the nobleman, "I have heard that you collect the finest teas and tea ware in the world. May I share a cup of tea with you?"

The nobleman was surprised, since the beggar did not

look like someone who would be able to appreciate the intricacies and delicacies of fine tea, but not wanting to appear rude, he agreed and asked that one of his best teas be brewed in one of his finest teapots. The beggar took a few sips, then looked disappointed and said to the nobleman, "The tea is fine, but it may be that the teapot is simply too new to bring out the fullest flavor of the tea. A teapot of several decades must be used to be worthy of this tea."

And then the beggar pulled out his only possession, a fine, well-used Yixing teapot. The story ends with a fine cup of tea, brewed in the Yixing pot, shared by the two men, who, from that point on, become friends and shared tea together every day for many years.

TEA'S INFLUENCE ON ASIAN ARTS

Tea played a significant part in the development of the East Asian arts. Beginning in the thirteenth century and lasting for hundreds of years, there was a large and enthusiastic market for fine utensils, particularly fine ceramics, to be used in the brewing and serving of tea in Japan, China, and Korea.

The tea ceremony in seventeenth-century Japan became a way for noblemen to display their wealth or power and to

"Ecstasy is a glass of tea and a piece of sugar in the mouth."
—*Alexander Pushkin*
(1799–1837)

Tea in Russia

In the 1600s, a trade route was developed between China and Russia. The route was long and difficult, as the paths went through treacherous mountainous terrain and barren countryside for a distance of about eleven thousand miles. It took Chinese traders approximately sixteen months to make the journey to Russia, so all products brought from China were expensive and considered luxury items in Russia, including tea.

There is some controversy about just when tea first came to Russia, but most scholars date the event to 1618, when the emperor of China sent a gift of several chests of tea to the Czar Alexis.

In spite of its great cost, tea became immensely popular with the royalty and high society of Moscow. It took nearly a century for the price of tea to drop, but when it did, the general populace became equally enthusiastic about the beverage. The Russians were quick to develop their own way of blending different teas together. On the whole, they pre-establish their social standing within the community. One of the greatest proponents of this was Hideyoshi, who had a great love of Korean pottery. In 1592 (only a year after he commanded his tea master, Rikyu, to commit ritual suicide), he sent warships to Korea and brought back fifty

ferred strong, dark tea sweetened with honey, sugar, or jam.

Typically, two or three different kinds of tea were brewed in individual pots, then small but concentrated amounts of the infusion were poured into a single cup. Hot water was added to dilute the concentrated liquid, the quantity depending on personal preferences.

The water was heated in a samovar, a large kettle first used in the eighteenth century, patterned after those used in Mongolia as early as the thirteenth century. The samovar consisted of a large kettle (usually copper or bronze), a tap, and a charcoal burner as a heat source. A cylindrical pipe of hot air passed through the water-filled container to heat the water and keep it an even temperature. During the warm summer months, the samovar was placed outside in the garden. In winter, it was brought into the house, where a long pipe carried the smoke directly into the chimney. The water was deemed ready for tea when the samovar began to make sounds. According to tradition, the water is ready after it "sings," but before it "growls."

Tea was served in a glass, and wealthy Russians used a silver or bronze holder, decorated with engraved pictures, to hold the heat-tempered tea glass. Called *podstakanniki*, which literally means "under the glass," these are still in use today.

Russians generally ate only one large meal a day, usually between three and six in the afternoon, but they would drink tea all day long. A cup of tea, whenever it was taken, was usually served with sweets—cakes and cookies. Rather than putting a sweetener *in* the tea, it became customary to take a spoonful of jam or a lump of sugar in the mouth, followed by a mouthful of hot tea, flavored with citrus.

Teas that are commonly called "Russian teas" were actually China teas such as Keemun, Chingwoo, Szechwan, and Lapsang souchong, blended together and sweetened with spices and citrus.

Korean potters to make the ceramics he wanted. This was the first of the Japanese invasions of Korea—others followed in 1597 and 1598—that were eventually called the "pottery wars."

Of course, Hideyoshi wanted more than pots. His ultimate goal was to dominate the Koreans and to force them to help him overtake the Chinese throne in Beijing. China sent troops to Korea to prevent this, and the combined Chinese and Korean forces were winning the war against the Japanese when Hideyoshi died suddenly in September 1598, apparently of a heart attack. The Japanese gave up the fight and returned home.

The results in Korea of these pottery wars were devastating. Economic hardship was widespread, and only the wealthy aristocrats and scholars could afford to drink tea during the years following these wars. Tea drinking and the tea ceremony were only reestablished in Korea in the early nineteenth century under the direction of the scholar Tasan Chong Yak-yong (1762–1836), who began the practice of drinking tea in a formal way in a special tearoom.

Korean Potters

Most of the Korean potters brought to Japan were taken to the port city of Karatsu, in eastern Japan. Here, in the seventeenth century, they introduced the *noborigama*, the chambered "climbing kiln," which greatly impacted the Japanese ceramics industry by opening up the possibility of creating many different types of glazes. The huge

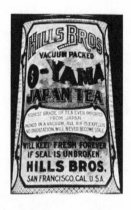

The first vacuum-packed tea, 1900; "will keep fresh forever if seal is unbroken"

kilns used massive amounts of firewood, and the resulting ash created beautiful colors and glazes on the pottery. The pottery coming from this district was called Karatsu ware and was characterized by freehand or geometric patterns from nature, painted on a white background.

Raku Ware

Different potters, of course, developed different styles, some of which were forgotten as soon as they developed, while others, such as raku, are still remembered and revered today. Raku ware, a lead-glazed earthenware, was first created in the sixteenth century in Kyoto, specifically for making vessels for the tea ceremony. Many consider raku the most remarkable of all tea pottery.

Tanaka Chojiro, the son of one of the Korean potters taken to Japan, made bowls that were simply shaped, with a basic monochrome glaze, usually either black or dark

"If this is coffee,
bring me tea. But
if this is tea, please
bring me coffee."
—*Abraham Lincoln*
(*1809–1865*)

brown. This was in keeping with the aesthetic of wabi, held so important by the tea master Rikyu. The bowls were originally called *ima-yaki*, meaning "now wares," but the name was eventually changed when Hideyoshi awarded Chojiro an honorary gold seal with the name *Jurakudai*, the name of his palace, which eventually came to symbolize his rule. Chojiro was probably greatly honored to receive this accolade from the ruler, but he eventually shortened the name to raku, which literally means "joy" or "happiness." He not only used the name for his pottery, but also adopted it as the family name.

Today, Kichizaemon Raku maintains the family tradition and represents the fifteenth generation to do so.

Oribe

By the end of the sixteenth century, art in Japan had undergone a transformation, due in part to the creative genius of the tea master, scholar, and gentleman samurai Furuta Oribe (1544–1615).

Oribe, who had been one of Rikyu's students, was one of the first tea masters appointed by the emperor after his teacher's death. Among his other skills, Oribe was also a stunningly innovative artist who showed great creativity in creating ceramics to be used in the tea ceremony. He completely changed the type of glaze used on traditional pottery, and his wares were used not only for formal tea ceremonies but for more casual, domestic occasions as well.

His ceramics featured thick glazes of brilliant green, pink, and black. He was able to attain such a stunning, glistening effect that his pottery shone like glass. The graphic motifs found on his pottery were painted on with an iron glaze, creating an almost modernistic appearance. Many of the motifs were exotic for Japan, showing for the first time the influence of the West.

A label from a tea chest of Java tea shipped to Amsterdam (1835)

CHAPTER 7

Tea Spreads Throughout the World

"Goodness is a decision for the mouth to make."

—*Lu Yu, eighth-century tea master*

CHINA ISOLATES HERSELF

Although historical events in China during the fifteenth, sixteenth, and seventeenth centuries had little direct impact on the story of tea, they form a chapter that cannot be ignored, for these events formed the foundation for the tremendous impact tea was to have on the world—and particularly on China—during the eighteenth and nineteenth centuries.

The Ming dynasty lasted 276 years, under the rule of sixteen different emperors. It was a time in Chinese history during which arts and culture were emphasized, and there was great enthusiasm for maritime exploration. During the early fifteenth century, China amassed the most powerful naval force ever assembled in the world, and one that was larger than any other until modern times. Under the leadership of an Admiral Zheng, Chinese ships went to present-day Vietnam, Java, Sumatra, Sri Lanka, and the east coast of Africa. Tea proved to be a popular trade item wherever these ships traveled. By the middle of the century,

"What would the world do without tea?—
how did it exist?"
—*Sydney Smith* (*1771–1845*),
English writer and clergyman

however, Chinese shipbuilding and exploration came to an abrupt halt, for no clear and apparent reason. The cause was perhaps economic, but the change may also have been due to the personalities of the new rulers of the country.

During the fifteenth century, the Ming dynasty was under attack from both the Mongols and the Japanese. Rather than fight back, the Chinese government's response was to retreat from the world. By the end of the 1430s, China imposed a policy of "strength through isolation." The result was a very strong, complex central government that provided stability for its citizens, but its rigidity could not weather the changes that would eventually lead to the decline of the ancient Chinese civilization.

At the same time that the Ming rulers were isolating themselves, Europe was undergoing a state of unrest that resulted in the dynamic transformations of the Renaissance, the Reformation, growth of national states, and expansion into the New World.

While the West was experiencing unprecedented and rapid changes and becoming more and more enamored with progress and the future, China's motto at this juncture was "change within tradition," which meant a resistance to outside influences and a tendency to idealize the past.

The result was that China fell far behind the West in terms of warfare, technology, material culture, and economic and political organization. All of this set the stage for Western expansion into and domination of a China that could not fight back on equal footing, either physically or psychologically.

EUROPEAN TRADE ROUTES TO ASIA

In Europe, the sixteenth century dawned with great excitement over sea trade and exploration. Vasco da Gama, in 1497, had rounded the Cape of Good Hope in southern Africa and landed in India, opening up great possibilities for trade with the East—and paving the way for the flow of tea from Asia to Europe that would eventually follow. Before da Gama's epic journey, trade between Europe and the East had been limited to overland routes, with most caravans starting in Vienna. The journey eastward to Asia was long and dangerous, but there were great riches to be made by bringing back exotic luxury items such as silks and spices to wealthy Europeans. Tea, at this point, was not a trade item and did not appear in Europe until a century later.

As the sixteenth century progressed, Portugal, with her superior ships and navy, continued to develop sea trade routes and, for many years, held a monopoly on these ocean paths. In 1542, the Portuguese began trading with Japan. Finally, in 1557, after years of petitioning, they were granted permission from the Chinese government to set up trading posts, called "factories," on the rocky point of Macao, where it juts into the Pearl River (now known as the Zhujiang River) as it joins the China Sea.

The first European to encounter tea and report back what he had experienced was the Portuguese Jesuit Father Jasper de Cruz, in 1560. Father de Cruz was a missionary on the first commercial trading trip to China after Portugal was granted trading privileges

Many European missionaries were allowed to live permanently in China, for they were learned men who proved to be irresistibly interesting to Chinese scholars. In return, the Jesuits were greatly influenced by the Buddhist monks with whom they came in contact. They were particularly impressed with the large quantities of tea drunk by the monks for their use in their meditation practice. Once again, religion plays a major role in the story of tea, for as the Jesuit missionaries wrote about this marvelous, exotic beverage, their words spread throughout Europe, and many eagerly awaited their first taste of tea.

TEA IN EUROPE

The British were preoccupied with their expansion to the New World and were slow to enter the Pacific trade. But on December 31, 1600, Elizabeth I granted a charter to the John Company, which was eventually to be known as the British East India Company. The primary purpose of the formation of this company was the promotion of Asian trade "for the honor of the nation, the wealth of the people, the encouragement of enterprise, the increase of navigation, and the advancement of lawful traffic," as the charter stated.

The trademark of the East India Company; c. 1600

This chartered company functioned as a business under the direct control of the sovereign state of Britain. The company was able to combine a sharp business acumen with the political strength of the state to become a powerful organization. Its power would prove to be extremely lucrative for both the investors of the company and the British government, but for both the Indians and the Chinese it would prove to be a devastating power to confront.

The British East India Company lost no time in trying to carry out its mission. The first ships sailed to the Far East in 1601, others followed in 1604 and 1607, then every year until 1615. The British established factories in India, Siam, Sumatra, Java, and Japan. In spite of persistent efforts, however, the British were unable to establish trading relationships with China for many years.

Portugal and Holland, which were closely associated politically during the sixteenth century, shared the profits and risks of their trading ventures. This partnership dissolved in 1602, when Holland formed the Dutch East India Company—organized along the lines of the British East India Company—and continued in her Pacific trade alone.

In 1609, the Dutch East India Company established trade with Japan and was allowed to build a factory in Hirado, in the southwest part of the country. From here, the Dutch not only bought Asian wares to take back to Europe, but also, for a while, supplied the Japanese with Chinese goods.

Even though Europeans had heard about tea for decades, it wasn't until 1606 that it first came to Europe as an item of trade, in the port city of Amsterdam. At this point, and for many years to come, tea in Europe was found only in apothecary shops. At first, it was nothing more than a novelty, but by 1610–1611 it had become a regular item of trade for both Holland and Portugal.

Tea acquired its first popularity in the Dutch capital, The Hague, even though it was quite expensive. In spite of the initial enthusiastic response, however, the demand for tea in Holland gradually declined, and by 1647 prices had begun to fall drastically.

But there was a ready and growing market elsewhere. For example, by the middle of the seventeenth century, it had become quite fashionable in Paris to drink tea. Tea's Parisian popularity was chronicled by Madame de Sévigné (1626–1696), whose letters paint a fascinating picture of Paris in the mid-seventeenth century. Madame de Sévigné is credited with starting the custom in Europe of drinking tea with milk.

TEA IN ENGLAND

The first twenty years of the British East India Company charter were not very successful in Asia, largely because Asian trade was dominated by Dutch, and to some extent still by the Portuguese.

"Tea has been one of the saviors of mankind. I verily believe that, but for the introduction of tea and coffee, Europe might have drunk itself to death."

—Sir James Crichton-Browne, M.D., former president of the London Medical Society, April 1915

It wasn't until 1657 that the Dutch first to brought tea to London. The first advertisement for tea appeared in the British weekly magazine the *Mercurius Politicus*, in September of 1658: "That Excellent, and by all Physitians approved, China Drink, called by the Chineans, Tcha, by other Nations Tay alias Tee, is sold at the Sultaness-head, a Cophee-house in Sweetings Rents by the Royal Exchange, London."

Although the British love affair with tea eventually became legendary, its popularity was not immediate. Paralleling the situation in The Hague, tea in London was at first considered a medicine, and it was found primarily at apothecaries. Soon, however, as the advertisement indicates, it was also available in coffeehouses, the small restaurants where coffee and tea were served, and people (mostly men) gathered for conversation. Samuel Pepys wrote in September 1660, only three years from tea's first introduction to London, "I did send for a cup of tee (a China drink) of which I never had drank before."

Because the Dutch East India Company had such tight

The London Gazette.

Publiſhed by Authority.

From Monday December 13. to Thursday December 16. 1680.

Lisbon. Nov. 11.

THe Court is gone to *Alcentara*, and will remain there all this month; the Queen and the Infanta being very much delighted with the place, We are expecting here the Marqvis de Dronero, who comes in the quality of Ambaſſador Extraordinary from the Duke of *Savoy*, to demand the

Advertiſements.

THeſe are to give notice to Perſons of quality, That a ſmall parcel of moſt excellent TEA, is by accident fallen into the hands of a private Perſon to be ſold: But that none may be diſappointed, the loweſt price is 30 s. a pound, and not any to be ſold under a pound weight: for which they are deſired to bring a convenient Box. Inquire at Mr. Tho Eagles at the Kings Head in St. James's Market.

A 1680 newspaper advertisement for tea

control over the tea trade, no tea was imported by the British East India Company until 1669. The result was that the price of tea remained quite high in England for many years. In 1664 a pound of tea cost about two pounds sterling. Considering that a footman only earned between two and six pounds a year, the cost of tea was steep indeed.

Catherine of Braganza

In spite of the high cost, tea's popularity took a giant leap forward when the Portuguese princess Catherine of Braganza and Charles II of England married in 1662. Both Charles, who had grown up in the Dutch capital where tea was readily available, and his new Portuguese wife were confirmed tea drinkers, and they are credited with introducing tea to the royal court in England. Drinking tea quickly became associated with royalty and the upper class.

Before Catherine came to court, most people in England who were drinking tea were doing it for medicinal pur-

Catherine of Braganza

poses, rather than for its taste. Even though the Japanese and the Chinese were finding tea delicious by the mid-seventeenth century, the teas brought to Europe from Asia were of inferior quality and taste, and most Europeans did not know how to brew them to extract the sweetest flavors. Catherine was to change all that, however, for she sought out the best teas available and taught the English ladies how to brew tea that was quite pleasurable to drink.

Catherine's influence on England was not only immediate and domestic, but long-lasting and far-reaching as well. Portugal was faced with great competition from the Dutch for trade in the East. Nevertheless, it was still a quite wealthy country, as reflected by Catherine's wedding dowry. Catherine brought five hundred thousand pounds in ready cash, but more importantly, the marriage union opened up new trade routes, as England was granted free trading rights in Brazil and the Portuguese East Indies. Tangiers and Bombay were thrown into the pot as well, and control of these islands passed to England. Catherine, by nature of her dowry, became an important link between England and Asia.

As a direct consequence of the marriage and the dowry, the British also gained an even stronger foothold in India and made Bombay its base of operations. The British East India Company was granted a new charter from the king that gave it a complete monopoly over all trade and commerce in China and India.

During the latter half of the seventeenth century, tea continued to be more of a novelty for the aristocracy than anything else. By 1675, however, it could also be purchased in food stores, and its popularity continued to grow steadily until, by the end of the seventeenth century, most of the British middle and upper classes were drinking tea daily. It was still expensive, however, and for the working class, tea remained a luxury.

At this point, both black and green tea were being shipped to England. By most accounts, the British imported forty thousand pounds of tea in 1699, and much of this popularity can be attributed to the availability of sugar. Tea, coffee, and chocolate are all inherently bitter, and the addition of sugar to all these exotic imports made them much more palatable. The upper and middle classes, who could afford it, used refined white sugar,

Fig. 13 Evolution of the Teacup

while the lower classes drank less-expensive, poor-quality tea mixed with coarse brown sugar or molasses. A cup of high-quality, sweetened tea was an unusual treat for most people.

In spite of the addition of sugar, tea gradually lost its appeal in France, as wine, chocolate, and coffee gained ground. Its popularity continued to grow in England, however, and, unlike the French, the English gradually began to adopt tea as the beverage of choice at social gatherings, rather than alcohol.

Coffeehouses and Tea Gardens

By 1714, when George I became king, there was great interest in tea. Britain's great literary figure of the late eighteenth century, Dr. Samuel Johnson (1709–1784), a famous frequenter of coffeehouses, was an early advocate of tea as well. He wrote, "with tea amuses the evening, with tea solaces the midnight, and with tea welcomes the morning." He also wrote, "Tea's proper use is to amuse the idle, and relax the studious, and dilute the full meals of those who cannot use exercise, and will not use abstinence." These were fine and stirring words for tea enthusiasts.

Johnson was not the only one to wax poetic over tea. The dramatist Colley Cibber (1671–1757) wrote in his play *The Lady's Last Stake*, act 1, scene 1, "Tea! Thou soft, sober, sage and venerable liquid; thou female tongue-running, smile smoothing, heart opening, wink-tippling cordial, to whose glorious insipidity I owe the happiest moment of my life, let me fall prostrate."

With a growing demand for tea, more merchants began to carry it in their establishments. Thomas Twining opened a teahouse in 1717 next to his coffeehouse on the Strand. The establishment was remarkable for a couple of reasons: (1) he was serving tea and not coffee, and (2) he allowed unchaperoned ladies to purchase tea for themselves—a revolutionary idea. Before this innovation, a woman had to send her husband or servant to purchase tea (or anything else) for her, or at least have a male accompany her.

Twining continually worked to improve the taste of the tea blends and varieties that he sold. Playing on the sensibilities of the class-conscious British, he advertised his company as "suppliers to the nobility and gentry" and named his new teahouse The Golden Lyon. By 1734, Twining had decided that there was a fortune to be made in tea, and he gave up the coffeehouse to concentrate on tea.

The origins of London's private "gentlemen's clubs" can be seen in these coffeehouses where men gathered to drink tea and coffee, discuss business and politics, or simply visit with friends. Throughout the country, members of the working class went to pubs and taverns to drink tea (and ale), but those who lived in London could also go to pleas-

Thomas Twining

ure gardens or tea gardens to enjoy a cup. Many of these were rowdy places with dancing, games, fireworks, boat rides, Indian jugglers, equestrian entertainments, and circus acts. A few of the more sedate and sophisticated pleasure gardens were for the upper class, however, and women and children of the gentry were allowed to go to these.

The most famous pleasure garden in London was Vauxhall, which opened in 1732. Here, men and women could stroll along beautifully landscaped promenades and enjoy tea and tidbits in a pleasant, social setting.

By 1790, most of the pleasure gardens had closed, but tea, at home and in coffeehouses, teahouses, pubs, and taverns, had become an essential part of life for nearly everyone. It is estimated that laborers were spending approximately 10 percent of their food budget on tea and sugar. Tea with bread and cheese was the main meal of the day for the poor and the working class.

The teapot, elegant or plain, was an important household fixture by the end of the eighteenth century. It held an honored place in both stately mansions and humble cottages and became a symbol of the British love affair with tea, one that crossed class and geographic lines and united people throughout the country.

Why did the British prefer tea to coffee, unlike the rest of Europe? The influence of the East India Company cannot be overlooked. Because the government had granted the company a monopoly, vast fortunes were made in the tea trade, and the men who stood to gain the most were the most enthusiastic about creating the tea craze. The British

Vauxhall Gardens, 1751

East India Company had been, for all intents and purposes, forced out of the Mediterranean trade by the French and Dutch, so it was difficult for them to get coffee, which came from primarily from Arabia and Ethiopia, but thanks to the booming Asian trade, they did have a steady supply of tea.

But the drink and the etiquette surrounding it also appealed to the British. They loved it because it was exotic, because it was such an important commodity for their own British East India Company, because it conveyed an aura of something more than just a cup of hot beverage. In the end, who knows precisely what causes fads and fashions, and what causes a fad to become a habit? The British taste for tea, a commodity no longer exotic or aristocratic, is so ingrained within the culture that it has lasted for centuries. It must have more than mere fashion to recommend it!

THE PATH OF TEA—FROM CHINESE MOUNTAINTOP TO ENGLISH TABLETOP

Canton

The eighteenth century, which was an exciting time of expansion and discovery for Europeans, and of course particularly the British, was a period of decline in China. Their persistence in traditional patterns made the Chinese resistant to an exchange with the West, whether the exchange was of trade goods or ideas. China's sense of its own superiority to all foreigners included the Western nations. The general feeling in China was that their ruler was the most powerful in the world, that their history was the longest and most noble, and that people of all other nations were inferior and unworthy of diplomatic exchange.

Nevertheless, in 1685, the emperor of the Qing dynasty (1644–1911), K'Ang Hsi, decided to open all ports (with stiff duties to safeguard Chinese interests) to Europeans. In 1715 this decision was revoked, however, and all ports except Canton were closed to foreigners as, once again, China turned inward. Trade between China and Europe was restricted to Canton for 160 years. The reasoning was straightforward—it was simply easier for the Chinese to control trade from one location than to try to control several different ports.

These directives, not surprisingly, caused Canton to become a very busy and active trading center in 1715. Not only the British but also the Dutch, French, Danish, and Swedish traded there, as well as merchants from India and the United States (after 1784), but it was the British who dominated trade in Canton.

Although the Portuguese and Dutch had done much to establish early trade routes, it was the British who persisted and who remained to take full economic advantage of the trade relations they had established.

The British quickly learned that trading with the Chinese was different from trading with any other country. For one thing, China did not need or want any of the goods that the Europeans had to offer. The Chinese were self-sufficient and showed little interest in Western trade items. They wanted only silver in exchange for the tea, silk, spices, and porcelain exported to England and other parts of Europe.

Enormous amounts of silver were being taken from South America and Mexico during this period, and this was shipped to China to pay for luxury trade goods.

The Eight Regulations

Because China remained in a superior trading position, the British were forced to obey what became known as the Eight Regulations. These rules controlled the lives of all foreign traders in Canton, both publicly and privately. Canton is located at the mouth of the Pearl River, where, according to the regulations, warships were not permitted at all. Trade ships had to anchor, load, and unload at the walled city of Whampoa, thirteen miles below Canton. Factories (places of trade) could only be built in specified areas located outside Whampoa, and no women or firearms were allowed inside the factory. No foreigners were allowed within the city walls, and traders could live only in the factories and only during the active trading season from June to December. When the ships left at the end of the year, all Westerners had to leave with them.

There were restrictions on travel, on free time and recreation, on mixing with the Chinese, on almost every aspect of life. But the traders with the East India Company persevered, for, in spite of everything—the frustrations, the regulations, and the difficulties—they were making fortunes buying and selling silk, spices, porcelain, and particularly tea.

Perhaps the regulation that had the greatest influence, in the long run, was that all orders and purchases had to be made through the Hong merchant guild, the Chinese-government-approved wholesalers, also known as the Co-Hong. The greed of both the European and the Chinese traders, coupled with the corruption of the Hong, was to prove to be a deadly combination for China.

Tea Found Only in China

China remained the only place in the world that exported tea, and the Europeans were determined to keep this trade open. European investments in tea during the early seventeenth and the eighteenth centuries involved a great gamble. The profits could be astronomical, as could the losses. Part of the difficulty and uncertainty lay in getting the tea from the mountains of interior China to the ports of England. The path was long, and misfortune could occur at any time.

Tea was grown by farmers with small plots of land in many different places in China, but wherever it grew, there were three main harvest times. The first, which produced the best quality of tea leaves, was from mid-April to June. The second and third pluckings (leaf harvests) were done later in the summer.

After the leaves were plucked, a process that was always done by hand (and still is, for the better-quality teas), farmers took their crops to a local merchant, who tested them for quality to make sure that they were not moldy and that they had been processed correctly. He then bought the leaves and bundled them together into a "chop." A chop consisted of bundles or chests of tea leaves all processed in the same way, to make the same kind of tea. The chop was not an absolute measure but was usually made up of a little over six hundred chests of tea. The chops were carried across the mountains by "coolies" (laborers), a journey that tested the strength and fortitude of even the most strong and determined individuals.

In this way, enormous amounts of tea reached distribution centers, where dealers, both Chinese and European, tasted and argued and negotiated until they had purchased the kinds and amounts of tea they desired. The tea was then put on boats to be taken down to Canton on the Pearl River.

From the tea shrubs to the tea ships was a journey that took up to six torturous weeks, usually through rain and humidity. It was as far as twelve hundred miles to Canton from some of the more remote tea plantings, and the only path went through mountainous and difficult terrain. The coolies carried backbreaking amounts of tea—some accounts say up to 300 pounds (136 kilograms) per person. Ernest Henry Wilson, the great British plant collector, wrote, "With their huge loads they are forced to rest every hundred yards or so, and as it would be impossible for the carrier to raise his burden if it were once deposited on the ground he carries a short crutch, with which he supports it when resting, without releasing himself from the slings."

In spite of the difficulties, by September, the goods were usually at the ports. At Canton, European tea agents (men hired by the traders for their expertise in choosing the highest-quality teas) made their selections, and finally, in late fall or early winter, the ships set sail for Europe—a sea journey that could take several months.

After unloading the tea, silks, and spices, the traders indulged in a brief rest, then started the process all over again. The best time to begin the four-month journey to Canton from London was April, to take advantage of the summer weather. Even though this meant lying in a Chinese port waiting for the tea to come in for several months, it was preferable and much safer than trying to come in during the fall.

Bohea, a black tea, was considered the coarsest and cheapest. Congo and pekoe were both more expensive and higher-quality black teas. Hyson was thought of as a fine green tea, and imperial was a medium-quality tea.

Because tea was so expensive and because it was sold loose out of barrels, unscrupulous merchants sometimes added filler to bulk up the tea and make it look as if customers were getting more for their money. Anything and everything was tried, from vegetable to mineral. It was easier to taste adulterants in green tea than in black tea, and this may have been a factor in the growing preference for black tea in England.

"Secondhand" tea was also available. Tea was so expensive that it was not uncommon for maids in wealthy homes to take the used tea leaves left over from a meal and to dry and resell them.

"Monkeys Gathering Tea in China. Fanciful picture illustrating an early legend. After Marquis, 1820." From W. H. Ukers' 1935 classic *All About Tea*

Eighteenth-Century Teas

The finest teas produced in China in the eighteenth and nineteenth centuries were not sold to foreigners, but were reserved for the Chinese emperor and the high court. Some of these were called "monkey-picked tea," a name that apparently originated in the eighteenth century. Monkey-picked Ti Kuan Yin oolong tea was discovered in Fujian Province, and legend says that the trees were so high, monks trained monkeys to pick the leaves. The tea made from these leaves was so fine that only the emperor (Qian Long, who ruled from 1735 to 1795) and nobles of the court were allowed to drink it. As it became more available, it was drunk by the general populace. The name and the surrounding legend have provided inspiration for poets, artists (and merchandisers!) throughout the centuries, our own time not excepted.

At the end of the eighteenth century, people in Britain were drinking black tea almost exclusively. There were about twenty different teas and tea blends available (compared to the fifteen hundred that the U.K. Tea Board says are available today), including:

Bohea (Bohea dust and Bohea with pekoe)
Pekoe
Imperial
Bloom and imperial
Congo (Congo with pekoe, Congo with Bohea)
Green tea (green dust, green with imperial)
Bloom green
Finest hyson

TAXES AND SMUGGLING
IN THE EIGHTEENTH CENTURY

From the first importation of tea, beginning when the British East India Company first established a factory at Canton, the British government imposed a tax on it. The amount of tax on tea varied widely over the centuries, and brought enormous revenues to the British government. Even at the beginning, the tax on tea imported into England was five shillings per pound—equal to thirty-two British pounds today, or almost sixty dollars! Tea itself was costing about ten to twelve shillings a pound by the middle of the eighteenth century—a far cry from the two pounds sterling it cost a century earlier. In spite of the cost and the tax, there seemed to be an insatiable demand for tea throughout England, and people continued to purchase it in substantial quantities.

After 1750, the British import of tea had increased from three to over ten million pounds a year. Because the tea was so heavily taxed, the government was making huge profits from the tea trade, and, not surprisingly, a black market for tea quickly arose. Smugglers brought tea into England from wherever they could get it. Even though China was still the only place that produced tea, it was shipped to other ports, such as those in the East Indies, India, China, and Japan (via Holland). Smugglers bought the tea from all these places and took it to the southern coast of England, where it was loaded onto wagons and horses and immediately dispersed throughout the country.

By 1760, the tea trade was worth so much money that it became increasingly clear that the fortunes of Parliament and the British East India Company were inextricably intertwined. The rise or fall of one intimately affected the other. For example, in 1772, there was a revolt by the working class against paying the high taxes demanded on tea. As a consequence, the stock of the East India Company fell, only to be rescued by the government, which reduced the tea tax, at least temporarily. Alan MacFarlane, coauthor of *The Empire of Tea*, says that between 1711 and 1810, seventy-seven million pounds in *taxes* were collected from the tea trade—and one pound in 1800 was the equivalent of fifty pounds, or approximately ninety-four dollars in today's market. In 1800, one-tenth of all British import tax came from tea.

William Pitt, who was responsible for increasing the tax on tea in Britain in 1797, guessed that half the tea consumed in England was smuggled in. Tea was so popular by this time that the thought of doing without it was intolerable—as was the thought of paying the heavy taxes imposed by the government. From the late 1600s until the late 1700s, smugglers were very well organized and had the support of the common people (and many of the upper class as well). They were able to develop a good communication system and enjoyed great success selling their smuggled wares. The smugglers were so bold, so well connected, and so skilled that when their cargo was seized by the government and put into storage houses, they would simply steal it back and continue with business as usual.

Tea and European Decorative Arts

The growing popularity of tea, particularly among the upper classes, inspired a parallel growth in interest in all the accessories of tea. The eighth-century Chinese tea master Lu Yu had written about the twenty-four pieces necessary for tea in China, but the British managed to figure out even more accoutrements to use with tea, including silver and furniture as well as porcelain and pottery.

Queen Anne, who succeeded William and Mary at the beginning of the eighteenth century, used a silver tea set—a custom that was quickly copied by aristocratic ladies throughout the country. These English ladies found out, however, that silver teacups are uncomfortable to hold when filled with hot tea...not nearly as easy to hold as Chinese porcelain. As a result, the paper-thin, beautiful Chinese porcelain cups were in great demand and were considered the only true and appropriate way to take the drink. Of course, the silver tea service, consisting of the teapot, creamer, and sugar bowl, remained a symbol of wealth and refinement.

The Chinese were quite willing to sell tea wares of pottery and porcelain as well as tea itself. At first, however, they refused to sell the best-quality wares, keeping them for their own use. Better and better porcelain pieces eventually became available to European markets, and these and other Chinese wares were brought to England. As the wares

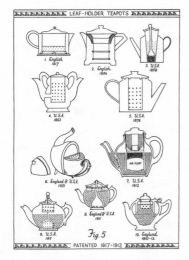

1. English 1817
2. English 1859
3. U.S.A. 1858
4. U.S.A. 1863
5. U.S.A. 1876
6. England & U.S.A. 1901
7. U.S.A. 1912
8. U.S.A. 1911
9. England & U.S.A. 1911
10. England 1910-12

Fig. 5

PATENTED 1817-1912

"Teas vary as much
in appearance as
the faces of men."
—*Hui Tsung (1082–1135),
Chinese emperor*

became more beautiful, the demand for them increased dramatically, until finally a mania for anything Chinese spread throughout Europe, particularly in England, during the middle of the eighteenth century.

Chinese artists began to make tea ware specifically for sale to England. They had invented hard paste porcelain and kept the secret of kaolin (the Chinese clay essential for creating porcelain) closely guarded for centuries, with the result that for quite a long time, Asian tea ware was superior to anything made in Europe. The first European porcelain was made in Meissen, Germany, in 1709. For many years, British artists tried to produce their own fine ceramics, but everything they produced cracked easily when filled with hot liquids. It wasn't until the dawn of the nineteenth century that Josiah Spode developed the first good bone china in England. This is a hybrid porcelain, made by adding calcined bone to a hard paste.

In response to the demand for Chinese wares, British artists began to copy Chinese art, and a style called "chinoiserie" developed. Chinoiserie style was an imitation of Asian decorative arts, though it was done from a Western perspective and made no attempt to adhere to the rules and standards of the original. By the end of the 1760s, the mania for chinoiserie had finally begun to ebb, giving way to gothic revival and neoclassic styles.

Teapots and Other Tea Ware

As noted earlier, the first vessels for brewing tea sent to Europe were probably the Chinese wine ewers. The first real teapots, however, were the prized Yixing pots from China, which were of unquestionable beauty and quality. Inevitably others of varying quality followed.

The first teacups in England were imported about the same time as tea. These looked more like bowls than teacups as we know them; they were small and had no handles, as the Chinese did not use handles on their cups. The diminutive size of the cups indicated that tea both in England and in China was still precious and considered a luxury item. The small size also suggested that the same tea leaves were used over and over again, to get as many cups of tea out of the leaves as possible. The concentrated space allowed one to gather the leaves together to reuse them.

The tea saucer was always shipped with the cups or bowls. The saucer was said to have been invented in seventh-century China. The discovery is attributed to the daughter of a military official, who used a small plate to cool tea before she offered it to her father. In many parts of the world, the saucer is still used this way, instead of functioning to catch any tea spilled from the cup, as we use it.

Almost everything that had to do with tea was shipped in from Asia, including teapots, milk pots, tea canisters, sugar dishes, cups, and saucers. The amount of porcelain brought from China to England during the seventeenth and eighteenth century was staggering. In 1980, a ship that had sunk in 1643 in the South China Sea was found to contain massive amounts of porcelain, including over eight thousand cups of various types, including stem and conical shapes. Excavations of the *Geldermalsen*, a ship that was wrecked in 1752, yielded forty thousand cups and fifty thousand saucers.

By the 1770s, matching tea sets could be ordered from China through the East India Company merchants. These were called breakfast sets and were composed of a teapot, a sugar box (including a lid), a small stand for the teapot, a milk pot (like a cream pitcher), and a dozen cups (still without handles). In 1775, the East India Company ordered eighty tea sets, along with twelve hundred teapots, two thousand covered sugar bowls, four thousand milk jugs, and forty-eight thousand cups and saucers.

Even with such enormous amounts of porcelain being imported, the British pottery industry began its own manufacturing of tea ware toward the end of the eighteenth century, and it was at this time that the European custom of placing a handle on a teacup became common. While cups for tea had single handles, cups used for hot chocolate—or by those who were weak or infirm—had two handles, one on each side. Larger teacups were used at breakfast, while smaller ones were used for afternoon tea. No matter what size the cup was, though, the saucer stayed the same size.

CHAPTER 8

The British in India, China, and Ceylon

"I don't care about immortality, just the taste of tea."

—Lu Tung, eighth-century Chinese poet

THE BRITISH EAST INDIA COMPANY established the first British factory (trading post) on the coast of western India in 1619. At first, traders believed that they could exchange British broadcloth for Indian goods, but they quickly found out that Indian textiles were of such high quality, there was little interest in buying European cloth. Undaunted, the company discovered that they could purchase Indian-made items cheaply and sell them in Great Britain for a profit— but reselling textiles did not bring nearly the profits that tea did. It had become obvious to the East India Company that if they were to maintain the tremendous profits to which they had become accustomed, the tea trade had to continue, and, if at all possible, grow. With the continuing frustrations of dealing with the Chinese, the British began looking for alternative methods of obtaining tea. The logical choice was India.

GAINING CONTROL IN INDIA

In many ways, it was easier to do business in India than in China. For one thing, India was closer to England geographically, and for another, the government rulers were easier to manipulate, as there was no strong central government.

India, during the late seventeenth and early eighteenth centuries, was only loosely joined under the control of Mughal leader Aurangzeb Alamgir (1618–1707). There had been fierce fighting between Aurangzeb and his brothers for control of the throne, and the result was a country divided and weakened. Most of the Indian leaders were not opposed to trade with Europe in the early part of the eighteenth century, but Aurangzeb justifiably feared that it would further weaken India, and he tried to put restrictions on the activities of the East India Company. The company fought these limitations and were intimidating enough to the native rulers that they eventually were able to build factories along the Indian coastline, in spite of local opposition.

India, like China, wanted only precious metal in exchange for their trade goods. This system remained tolerable to the British during the first half-century of trade, from 1720 to 1770, but then several factors changed the situation. Up until the time of the American Revolutionary War, most of the silver used by England had come from Central and South America. After the war, supplies from Mexico were essentially cut off, and inflation led to a rise in the cost of silver as well. Demand for Asian goods in Britain was on the increase, but the Indian textile trade was in decline, in part as a result of increased competition from a growing European textile industry. The directors of the

East India Company knew that changes had to be made, both in India and in China, if they were to keep their profit margins up.

Looking about for other trade opportunities, directors of the company seized upon the idea of growing poppies and selling opium. Much of the Indian countryside was well suited for growing the crop, and there seemed to be ample cheap labor for farming and processing it. What made this strategy particularly attractive was the ready and growing market for opium. The plan was simple; grow opium in India and trade it to China for tea.

The company set about implementing this idea with great zeal. They needed access to more land, and freedom from restrictions imposed by the Indian government, so they began with a push for more political control in India. The company actually had its own army, and in 1757 their officer Robert Clive won a decisive victory over Indian troops at the Battle of Plassey. In 1758, Parliament granted the East India Company a monopoly for producing opium in India. From this point on, India gradually changed from a trading partner to a British imperial colony.

With its increased political power, the company was able to force Indian farmers to dedicate more and more land to growing poppies, which meant that acres of land were used for the production of opium rather than food or cotton. The result was widespread hunger and an even greater decline of the Indian textile industry, all of which was devastating to the economy of India. The effects of opium were to prove even more demoralizing to China.

The close ties between the East India Company and the British government were significant to the history of tea, of England, of India, and of China. In 1784, the British Parliament passed the India Act, which divided control of the company between a Court of Directors and a Board of Control, made up of government officials. This act declared that the company could "levy war or make peace." The company, therefore, actually carried out the will of the British government. It was a way for the British government to circumvent international laws and agreements that would have restricted a government, but did not apply to businesses.

By the early 1800s, huge tracts of land in southern India were seized by the British East India Company, with the help and support of the British army. India's methods of fighting were no match for European military might. After Plassey came the Anglo-Maratha conflicts of 1803–1805 and the conquest of the Sikhs in 1848. Finally, in 1857, one hundred years after the Battle of Plassey, the Indian colonies became British Colonial India under full control of Britain.

It is estimated that Britain controlled about half of all the land in India during the first part of the nineteenth century. Heavy taxes were levied on the native people, and these funds were used to transport troops from Britain to India and to pay the salaries of company directors and other employees. The vast amounts of land controlled by the company were planted in a crop that was to alter both India and China forever—opium poppies.

Names for Tea

In 1762, Carl Linnaeus wrote the *Species Plantarum*, a list of all known plants of the time and their scientific names. According to this eighteenth-century list, tea was accepted in two genera—*Theus* and *Camellia*. Linnaeus also included *Thea viridis*, his name for "green tea plant," and *Thea bohea*, the "black tea plant"—not realizing that they came from the same shrub. In 1818, Robert Sweet, an English botanist, united *Theus* and *Camellia* into one genus and called it *Camellia*, as it is still called today. It wasn't until 1959 that the International Code of Nomenclature named the tea plant *Camellia sinensis*. The name *Camellia* came from a Moravian Jesuit named Georg Joseph Kamel (1661–1706), who studied Asian plants. The species name, *sinensis*, means "from China."

Other outdated names that are still occasionally found today include *Thea viridis*, *Thea sinensis*, *Thea bohea*, *Camellia theifera*, and *Camellia thea*.

Because the Europeans first imported Chinese goods through the Fujian port of Amoy (now known as Xiamen), many of the words they adopted had the pronunciation of the Fujian dialect. Among these was the word *te*, which quickly came to be known as tea in English, although it remained *cha* elsewhere in China.

When it first came to London, tea was known by a variety of names, including "tcha," "tay," and "tee." The first recorded use of the spelling "tea" was in a letter from an agent of the East India Company, in 1615. The ancient Chinese word *tai* was adapted in English as tea, in German as *thee* (now *tee*), in French as *tee* or *thé*, in Korean as *ta*, in Russian as *chai*, and in Swedish as *ta*. The Chinese word *cha* was used in Japan, Persia, and Portugal. The Indian word was *chai*.

INDIAN POPPIES FOR CHINESE TEA

Arab traders had actually introduced opium to China some time between the fourth and seventh centuries. There are records dating back to the eleventh century indicating that doctors had prescribed the drug for conditions such as insomnia, pain, and diarrhea. But for many centuries, opium was considered purely medicinal, and usage was not widespread. Once Westerners began trading at Canton, however, Europeans used both tobacco and opium as items to trade to the Chinese, and heroin usage, in particular, escalated. Opium proved to be an excellent item for trade. With their monopoly in India, the British had a seemingly endless supply, and they soon found that the Chinese were finally interested in taking something other than silver in trade for tea. As silver became more expensive and scarce, the East India Company brought more and more opium to China to trade for tea.

Alarmed at the potentially dangerous addictive quality of the drug, the Chinese government (under the Qing dynasty) passed an edict as early as 1729 forbidding opium use except for medicinal purposes. Enforcement of this law was minimal, however, and use of opium, and the heroin made from it, continued to increase, along with the growing imports from the East India Company. As the number of opium addicts grew, the Chinese government's response was to threaten the East India Company with a reduction in the amount of tea they were allowed to buy. It is important to remember that, at this time, all the tea produced in the world still came from China. England's insatiable thirst for tea and the boundless profits enjoyed by the East India Company and the British government made the thought of any decrease in the amount of tea imported from China intolerable.

In 1796, the East India Company complied, at least in theory, to the demands of the Chinese government and stopped selling opium directly to the Chinese in Canton.

Instead, they sold Indian opium to private English merchants in Calcutta. The merchants, without skipping a day of trading, brought the opium to China, thus maintaining the illegal trade. The difference was that the company could now deny any responsibility for wrongdoing, and the tea trade, as well as the opium trade, continued to grow, with the full knowledge of both the British government and the company officials.

Growing Addiction in China

The number of opium addicts grew astronomically in China during the eighteenth century, and the problem was widespread before the Chinese government and royal leaders realized how serious it had become. In 1799, the Chinese issued another imperial edict that banned the importation of opium. This time, the punishment included banishment or death, but addiction had taken hold of such a large part of the populace that the trade continued.

A new emperor, Tao Kuang, came to throne in 1819, and hostilities between foreign merchants and the Chinese authorities began to increase. In 1830, the horror of the situation was intimately revealed to the Chinese emperor when his son died of an opium overdose.

In 1830, China imported over 2.5 million pounds of Indian opium, and the trade in opium was even more lucrative than the tea trade. There were an estimated 12.5 million opium smokers in China by 1836.

The paths of opium, tea, and silver were inextricably intertwined. For decades, the British and other Western nations had poured Mexican silver into China to pay for tea and other commodities. Between 1800 and 1810, the British paid an estimated 983 tons of silver to the Chinese, primarily for tea. With the arrival of Indian opium, this flow of silver reversed. From 1830 to 1840, the Chinese traded 366 tons of silver to the British, primarily for opium grown in India but controlled by the British. At one time there were nearly one million people working in the Indian opium industry.

Not unlike drug trafficking today, the opium trade created astronomical profits. The British government not only knew about the illegal trade, they encouraged it, thus encouraging opium addiction as well. They were devastatingly successful at it, opening new ports along the Chinese coast and finding new addicts.

Americans, too, were involved in the opium trade in China. Since the Indian opium market was under the monopoly of the British East India Company, Americans bought opium in Turkey and shipped it to China. At its height, however, the American opium trade was only one-twentieth the size of the British.

Growing Tensions

As tensions between China and England escalated, the problem could be encapsulated in a single statement: both nations felt that they were the greatest power on earth. The British, at the height of their extraordinary expansionism, felt as if their king deserved honor and respect from all peoples throughout the globe. The Chinese, who believed that

"All I can say is that on a long march, and where troops are exposed to great hardships, a cup of Assam tea is one of the most sustaining and invigorating beverages a soldier could have."

—*Sir Annesley De Renzy,*
Army Surgeon General,
The Lancet, *London, 1908*

they were descended from the gods and that their emperor was the Son of Heaven, thought that all other people were inferior to them. It was these attitudes, as much as conflicts in trade and economics, that fueled the increasing tensions between the two nations.

According to their charter, the British East India Company was scheduled to give up their monopoly on trade with China in April of 1834. In spite of protestations by the company, other European trading nations insisted that the terms of the charter be upheld. Unwilling to give up its position of leadership in China, the British government decided to assign a diplomatic official to replace the ruling committee of the company. To this end, the British Cabinet created a Chief Superintendency of Trade in Canton and awarded consular status to this position.

Lord William Napier was the first to be chosen as chief superintendent. Although the British had awarded him consular status, the Chinese had not, and they refused to acknowledge him as a high-ranking diplomat. When Napier sent word to the Chinese court that he was coming to meet with officials, they responded that he must wait for the emperor to call for him.

Napier was incensed and sailed to Canton anyway. If he could not meet with the emperor, he stated, the only other person he would talk with was the viceroy, the highest-ranking officer of the Hong, the group of Chinese merchants who controlled foreign trade. Unfortunately, members of the Hong were notoriously corrupt and were often bribed to turn a blind eye to much of the dealings with Western traders, including and especially those in the opium trade.

The Chinese viceroy refused to see Napier, told Hong members to send him home, and threatened severe punishment if they did not. Napier, still expecting to be treated as a high-ranking diplomat, continued to wait in Canton. The viceroy retaliated by capturing a British factory. He demanded that all the Chinese workers be sent home and ordered Napier to leave the country. Finally, he dictated a severe reduction in the tea trade, to go into effect immediately, and ordered that these measures were to stay in place until Napier left Canton. Napier refused, and the situation continued to escalate until Napier became quite ill with a fever, from which he eventually died at the port of Macau.

The British did not give up, of course, but sent other officials to deal with the situation. The Chinese were desperately concerned about the rampant opium addiction in the country and were determined to stop the opium trade. In 1838, the emperor appointed a new official, Lin Tse-hsu, to oversee the opium problem. Lin was scrupulously honest and passionate about stopping opium addiction. He demanded the surrender of all opium held by foreign merchants. When the Western traders did not comply, he stopped all trade with Britain, blockaded factories, and arrested many of the corrupt Hong officials.

The British leader in Canton at this time was Captain Charles Elliot, who personally also opposed the opium trade. Elliot responded to Lin's actions by ordering the British merchants to hand over all the chests of opium they had on board their ships, some twenty thousand chests. Lin accepted and destroyed all the opium.

Both Elliot and the British traders believed that their government would cover their losses, but government officials felt otherwise. They were furious. Elliot had accrued a bill for about nine million Mexican silver dollars' worth of opium (one Mexican dollar was worth about £2.5 in the mid-nineteenth century, which is about £169, or $335, today). And, in addition, he had openly acknowledged the existence of the opium, and by doing so, inadvertently accepted official responsibility for the illegal trade.

The Opium Wars

The British response to the situation was to send warships to Canton, where they quickly and efficiently destroyed Lin's army, in 1840, thus beginning the first Opium War. For the Chinese, it was a devastating war from the very beginning.

Even though the Chinese had actually invented gunpowder, they had never experienced anything like modern warfare. Their guns were fixed, making aim most difficult and trajectory poor. Many of the cannonballs went only a short distance. Such weaponry was ineffective against the superior British guns and cannons, and the Chinese quickly fled. The British persevered and soon had control of Canton and other parts of China. Fearing an attack on the capital city of Peking and the end of the imperial regime, Chinese officials finally persuaded their own emperor to sue for peace.

The result was the Treaty of Nanking, signed on August 29, 1842. Terms of the treaty opened up the ports of Canton, Amoy, Foochow, Ningpo, and Shanghai and gave Hong Kong to the British in perpetuity. In addition, England was awarded a "most favored nation" status in China. The Chinese were forced to pay for the lost opium and the cost of the war. Although the British also tried to convince the Chinese to legalize opium, the Emperor stood firm, saying, "nothing will induce me to derive a revenue from the vice and misery of my people."

The Chinese were both defeated and devastated. Much of the populace was firmly in the clutches of opium addiction, the government was unstable, and the morale of the people was painfully low as they realized that their country, which they had believed to be invincible, had been defeated by a tiny island halfway around the world.

Thus, the illegal opium trade continued, as did the Chinese resistance to it. The British were far from satisfied

The poppy plant

with the Treaty of Nanking and were impatient to open more ports and to legalize opium. The result was a second Opium War in 1856. Again, the British won easily, and the Emperor was again forced to negotiate to save Peking, resulting in the Treaty of Tientsin, in 1858. Even more ports were opened to foreigners, and Christian missionaries were allowed in. Eventually, the Chinese did legalize opium, and England continued to export Indian opium to China until 1911.

The tea trade was unaffected by the wars and disputes during the 1840s and 1850s, and profits continued to rise as tea became more and more important in English daily life. In 1836, John Barrow wrote in the British *Quarterly Magazine*, "It is a curious circumstance that we grow poppy in our Indian territories to poison the people of China in return for a wholesome beverage which they prepare almost exclusively for us."

GROWING TEA IN INDIA

The British had been aware for decades that tea plants were indigenous to India. Native shrubs were found growing in Assam as early as 1778, and there were rumors that the Assamese drank tea. Joseph Banks, a British botanist who accompanied Captain Cook during his long third voyage between 1776 and 1780, wrote that he believed tea could be grown successfully in northern India. The British had long been interested in growing tea in India, but as long as the China trade offered such high profits, this interest remained only academic.

In 1823, the British trader Robert Bruce went to Assam, where he learned of the existence of tea plants and became fascinated with the idea of cultivating tea in India. In 1826, the British government, with the support of the East India Company, annexed the region of Assam. This area, consisting almost completely of the valley of the upper Brahmaputra River, was a harsh, inhospitable land, very flat, and for the most part only three hundred feet above sea level. High temperatures and humidity made conditions stultifying throughout the year. Although hardly ideal for human habitation, the climate proved excellent for growing a huge variety of plants, including tea.

Robert Bruce was soon joined by his brother, Charles, who was commanding troops in the Assam region. The two brothers were tireless in their attempts to grow tea and were finally successful enough to send samples of their plants to Dr. Nathaniel Wallich, botanist for the East India Company. Other British traders, equally interested in the possibilities of growing tea in India, had also sent samples from wild tea shrubs they had found. Inexplicably, Wallich was slow to confirm that these samples were actually the tea plant, but finally on Christmas Eve, 1834, he declared that, indeed, the samples were of the tea shrub, which we now classify as *Camellia sinensis* var. *assamica*, and that they must be indigenous to Upper Assam. He stated, "We are perfectly confident that the tea plant which has been brought to light, will be found capable, under proper management, of being cultivated with complete success for commercial purposes."

We know today that *Camellia sinensis* var. *assamica* is indigenous to many warm regions, including Assam, Burma, Thailand, Laos, Cambodia, and Vietnam. It grows much larger than the tea plants indigenous to China (*Camellia sinensis* var. *sinensis*) and can reach heights of seventeen meters (fifty-six feet) or more, but are kept pruned to a more manageable size in the tea gardens or plantations. These warm region tea plants have large leathery leaves, grow quickly, and live to be about forty years old.

Camellia sinensis var. *sinensis* grows only 5.7 meters (17 feet) high, although it, too, is kept pruned to a height of a little over one meter (three to four feet) in cultivation. It prefers the cool temperatures of high elevations between two and six thousand feet, has narrow, small leaves, and

Wind clocks kept tea offices in London aware of the prevailing winds and thus the status of their shipments

grows slowly. It is a hardy, long-lived plant that can last a century or more. It takes approximately twice as many harvested China variety leaves to equal the weight of the larger-leafed assam variety.

Although the Bruce brothers and others tried to grow both varieties in their region of India, not surprisingly, the assam variety proved to grow much better than the varieties indigenous to high elevations in China. In the future, however, the Chinese variety would prove to do exceedingly well in the mountain region of Darjeeling.

When the East India Company lost the monopoly on trade to China in 1834, their interest in growing tea in India escalated quickly. One of the employees of the company, George James Gordon, was sent to China to collect plants and seeds, and to find experts to teach the British plantation owners how to grow and process tea. This latter assignment was not an easy one, for China guarded its tea secrets obsessively. Gordon did manage to purchase three batches of tea seed, but was not allowed to be present when these were collected, packaged, and shipped. When they were unpacked in India, the quality of the plants and seeds was so inferior, or they had been packed so poorly, that nothing had survived.

In spite of the challenges presented by growing tea in India, Charles Bruce painted such a rosy picture of the possibilities in his letters that many people in London became extremely interested in the idea. A group of investors banded together to form The Assam Company in 1839.

Charles Bruce tried growing both tea varieties in many different ways on his plantations and searched continually for better information and expertise. It took him several years to cultivate the shrubs and actually process tea, but by 1840, Bruce had produced five thousand pounds of tea.

In trying to convince businessmen to invest in the Assam Company, Bruce pointed out that labor in India was cheap and that the "peaceful habits of the Assamese" made them particularly well suited to the work of growing and processing tea. He also mentioned, however, that relations with labor might be difficult, a casual remark that was to prove a monumental understatement. In spite of the warning about labor problems, his report fired such enthusiasm in England that many new investors joined the ranks of the Assam Company.

How to Grow It?

The Chinese government strictly prohibited Chinese citizens from divulging information about growing or processing tea. Anyone who offered information about tea or who sold tea plants or seeds to foreigners was severely punished. In spite of this, the British were successful in convincing or bribing a few Chinese tea masters to come to India—but with questionable results. These men were probably not true tea masters and proved to know little about growing and processing tea. They were also very uncooperative in working with the British in India.

Ignorance about how to grow and process tea was just the first of many problems on the tea plantations in India. The heat and humidity in Assam were almost unbearable for the workers. Mosquitoes and the diseases they caused, including malaria, were widespread. Many of the British planters not only mistreated workers, making them work long hours with insufficient amounts of food and water, but also proved to be dishonest and corrupt, absconding with company funds.

The directors of the Assam Company in England received little information about what was actually happening at the plantations in India. Plantation owners kept sending back optimistic reports, and the Assam Company directors kept sending more money.

By the middle of the nineteenth century, massive amounts of money had been poured into the project, even though there was little information about how the funds were being spent. All anyone knew for sure was that, for many years, the British tea venture in India had shown little profit.

But the lure of great profits seemed to make everything worthwhile. The directors of the British East India Company knew that, potentially, there were fortunes to be made in Indian tea, which certainly proved to be true. They determined that the key lay in learning more about how to grow the plants and how to process the tea. To this end, in 1848, the company hired the British botanist and plant hunter Robert Fortune (1812–1880) to go to China and find robust plants and accurate information.

Robert Fortune

Robert Fortune's first gardening job was working in the Edinburgh Royal Botanic Gardens, a position that left him with a lifelong fascination with plants. He first went to China to collect plants as an agent of the Royal Horticultural Society, in 1843, shortly after the Treaty of Nanking had been signed and many ports in China were opened to the West for the first time. Fortune left Britain aboard the ship *Emu*, arrived in Hong Kong four months later, and immediately sailed to Amoy. Arriving in early September, he found the town itself filthy and left quickly to go inland looking for plants.

Fortune apparently attracted a great deal of attention as he traveled the country. His journals from this time say that he was often surrounded by a couple of hundred curious locals, who wanted to know what he was looking for. At the end of September, he endured a harrowing sailing trip to Chusan, an island off the eastern coast of China, having heard that there were many new species of plant life there. In spite of almost losing his life on numerous occasions due to shipwrecks, bandits, and disease, he considered this leg of the journey well worth the risk because of the rich diversity of plants he found. He collected and brought back many plants that were new to the West, including what is now known as the Chusan palm.

It was on this initial trip to China that Fortune saw tea growing for the first time. As he studied the tea plants and the procedure of withering and drying the leaves, he became the first Westerner to realize that green and black tea come from the same plants, despite their very different tastes. As Fortune discovered, the variations are due to the process, not the plant. Green tea is unoxidized, while black tea is produced by oxidizing the leaves.

In June 1844, Fortune decided to travel to the forbidden city of Soochow (now spelled Suzhou), which was still closed to Westerners. This necessitated his traveling in disguise. By this point, he had become proficient in Mandarin, and by shaving his head except for a pigtail and adopting Chinese dress, he was able to pass himself off as a Chinese merchant. It's said that his disguise was so good that his British friends took some time to recognize him, when he returned to Shanghai. Fortune not only collected plants on all of his adventures, he also kept careful notes on the soils and climate, and paid particular attention to how tea was planted, harvested, and processed.

In August 1848, he made his second journey to China, sent this time by the East India Company. His goal was to find the best possible tea plants and seeds for transplanting and planting in India. He managed to collect and send twenty thousand tea plants to India, using four different

A drawing of a scene in Kiang-nan, Anwhei, China, from Robert Fortune's book *Visits to the Tea Districts of China and India* (1852)

ships to minimize the danger of losing all the plants to one possible catastrophe. Because he did not know whether or not the tea seeds would stay viable throughout a long journey, Fortune used the newly invented Wardian cases to germinate the seeds en route. The Wardian case, the invention of Dr. Nathaniel Bagshaw Ward, a London physician and amateur botanist, was a miniature glass greenhouse, much like a terrarium. It allowed plant explorers to immediately plant seeds they had collected, then return to their home ports with small plants, rather than bags of seeds that might not have survived many months or even years at sea.

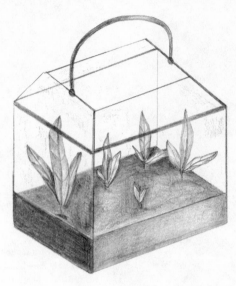

A Wardian case

Fortune was also able to hire eight Chinese tea experts to travel with him and to purchase implements and materials needed for processing the tea. The East India Company was ecstatic with his successful forays into China, and, on the basis of what he had learned in China, Robert Fortune was able to help tea production in India increase quickly and dramatically. Profits soon improved, and the Assam Company was able to pay its first dividend in 1853.

Robert Fortune went back to China between 1853 and 1856, sponsored this time by the United States government, which wanted to establish its own tea industry. The scheme was eventually abandoned, however, as a result of the onset of the American Civil War.

By 1862, two million pounds of tea were produced in India. In 1866, the amount had grown to six million pounds,

Darjeeling

Although most of the tea grown in India was still from the Assam region, other areas were experimenting with growing tea as well, and none was as successful, perhaps, as Darjeeling. In the mid-nineteenth century, Darjeeling was primarily a resort area, used by the British army and wealthy Indians as an escape from the heat of the lower-lying areas. Even though it is only 120 miles from Assam, no tea was grown there until 1856, when a British surgeon, Dr. Arthur Campbell, planted tea seeds in his botanical garden at Beech-wood, Darjeeling, at an altitude of seven thousand feet. Dr. Campbell and others quickly realized that the sinensis variety of tea (or *jat*, as it was called in Hindi) was better suited to growing in the cool climate of the mountainous regions of northern India than the assam variety.

The tea in Darjeeling proved to be of very high quality. It is said to have a "muscatel" flavor. Darjeeling tea was also found to be particularly good for blending with the scents and flavors of additives such as jasmine.

although 90 percent of the tea imported to England during this year was still from China. Although a great deal of tea was being produced in India, the production was very expensive, and the tea itself was of inferior quality. The banks and businessmen who had invested so heavily in Indian tea began recalling their loans, resulting in the—temporary—collapse of the Indian tea market in the late 1860s. After a few years, the tea industry was able to reorganize, and the result was increased production and better-quality tea, particularly from the Assam region. Eventually, Indian tea was sold more cheaply than that imported from China. In 1888, eighty-six million pounds of tea were produced in India, and imports from India finally surpassed those from China.

Nineteenth-Century Indian Tea Plantations

During the last half of the nineteenth century, the number of acres planted in tea in India grew astronomically, and with it, the need for labor. The Assam Company had begun to import labor from outside India as early as 1839, but as more and more land was planted in tea, the search for cheap labor centered on Bengal, where coolies were paid a small amount of money to leave their homes and go to Assam to work on the plantations.

Conditions on the journey from Bengal to Assam were horrible, with heat, mosquitoes, disease, and hunger plaguing the new workers. Labor contractors and agents were paid for each coolie whom they delivered alive to the tea plantations. "Alive" did not equate to "healthy," and in some years, over half of the coolies died in transit, while countless numbers arrived so weak that they died within the year, mostly from cholera. They were treated as just another part of the financial equation calculated by the Assam Company. If delivered alive, full payment was made. If a coolie died before reaching the plantations, payment was adjusted accordingly. About 30 percent of the recruits were women who brought children with them.

Why did these men and women voluntarily leave their homes, risk a harrowing journey, and work under devastating circumstances for very little money and almost no hope of returning home? They had no choice. Bengal at this point was suffering from a famine that resulted in the deaths, in 1865–1866, of almost 1.5 million people. Millions of others remained malnourished. It was a desperate situation from which there seemed to be no escape, except to take a chance on the tea plantations in India.

The British-controlled tea plantations in Assam during the nineteenth century were located far from one another. This geographic isolation allowed the owners to run their plantations as they desired. Like the slaves living on Southern plantations in the antebellum United States, all the tea workers lived on the plantation and were completely dependent on the plantation owners for housing, food, water, and medicine. Although some plantations were better than on others, in general, conditions on the plantations were devastatingly difficult for the workers. Heat and insects were relentless, and there was rarely enough food for the laborers. The water supplies were often polluted, and diseases such as malaria, fevers, diarrhea, dysentery, and cholera were rampant.

It was a situation from which there was no escape for the native worker. There are many records of workers being arrested and beaten severely for trying to leave the plantations. Through intimidation, through debt bondage, and through control of living quarters and food distribution, the British plantation owners held the native workers captive. As a result, the term "coolie," which originally meant "hired worker," is now considered offensive.

The situation was exacerbated by the intensity of the work required of the laborers. The planters were trying to accomplish the near impossible—the instant transformation of the Assam jungle into tea plantations. With their limited resources, they could only attempt this by forcing the coolies to perform extremely dangerous tasks, or by literally working them so hard and long that they died of exhaustion.

The Indian government, under the rule of the British, tried to protect the rights of the laborers with laws. Planters, fearful of a loss of profits, formed their own organization, called the Indian Tea Association, and became powerful enough to block any Indian reforms that would alter labor legislation.

By the end of the century, conditions had improved slightly, as the local Indian government within the tea districts gained strength and influence. But the real reason for the improved conditions was that much of the land had already been cleared, and the planters could turn their attentions to working the land already planted. This required labor that was tiring but not nearly as fatally exhausting as clearing land. Even so, conditions on the plantations remained hard. Plantation owners continued to refuse to provide enough food for the basic needs of the workers. Adults worked long hours, but often the only way a family could survive was to have children as young as five or six work alongside their parents.

By this time, half a million acres in India were planted in tea, almost half of which was found in Assam. The toil required to plant, grow, and process the tea caused the deaths of several hundred thousand coolies. But for all this toil and sacrifice, India was able to retain only 15 percent of the profits realized from these plantations—the remainder went to England.

Elephant clearing
jungle for tea estate
(India; undated)

The Essential Elephant

The Indian people were not alone in their suffering in the name of tea. The creation of the tea industry would not have been possible without elephants. These huge beasts were the only means, at first, of transporting the tea, and using elephants for power was the only way that the British could clear large parcels of densely forested land for planting. Even the elephants had a difficult time navigating through the Indian jungle. The result was an alarming decrease in the native elephant population, as hundreds of young elephants were captured and trained for working, and many did not survive. Today, the Asian elephant is ten times more at risk for extinction than the African elephant. This is the result, in part, of a loss of habitat. Their natural breeding and feeding grounds coincide with the land taken for tea plantations, and they have nowhere else to go.

Mechanization and Tea

The British learned much from the changes brought about by the Industrial Revolution in their own country, and they applied these lessons to improving production on tea plantations in India. The result was an efficient, mechanized method of farming tea whereby new agricultural methods were employed for the greatest yield possible. The plantations were huge, and the work force was now organized for optimum efficiency of production, with little regard for human need. This was dramatically different from the way the tea gardens and plantations were run in China, where production had really not changed for a thousand years.

The first mechanical hot-air driers were used in India in 1884. Formerly, the leaves had been allowed to air-dry or were roasted in pans over a fire. Soon, there followed a mechanized roll breaker to roll and twist the leaves, which had previously been done by hand. Finally, machines were invented to sort and pack the tea. The invention of the steam engine also increased profits from tea in India. Steamships carried processed tea down the Brahmaputra River, or steam-powered trains took it out of central Assam to the coast.

The combination of organized labor, steam power, mechanization, and good merchandising techniques helped boost production, increase the market, and lower the price of tea throughout the world. The result was that China simply could no longer compete on the world market, and China's tea trade began to decline after about 1890. The competition from tea grown in India had an impact on the lives of hundreds of thousands of the Chinese. For many centuries, the Chinese living in tea-producing regions had depended on the tea industry for their livelihood. When the Chinese tea market began to decline, many of these people lost their jobs, resulting in poverty and hunger. This situation contributed to the turbulence and instability of China during the latter nineteenth century.

TEA IN CEYLON

At end of the nineteenth century, the greatest competition to Indian tea was not from China but from Ceylon. Renamed Sri Lanka in 1972, Ceylon is a large tropical island only twenty miles off the southeastern coast of India. It is shaped like a teardrop, 270 miles long from north to south, and 140 miles across at its widest point. Arab and Chinese traders were well acquainted with Ceylon and traded frequently for the spices (especially cinnamon), pearls, and elephants found on the island.

Most of the country is at sea level or slightly above, but mountains in the center of the island rise eight thousand feet high. Although the northern and eastern parts of the country are in the "dry zone" and don't receive enough rainfall to grow crops on a large scale, the rest of the country is called the "wet zone" and receives one hundred inches of rain annually. Some isolated spots may even get up to two hundred inches, comparable to the amount of rain that falls on a rain forest.

The first Europeans to arrive in Ceylon were the Portuguese, who landed in 1505 and set up trading posts along the western coast. During the first half of the seventeenth century, the Portuguese and then the Dutch fought various tribal rulers of Ceylon, including the king of Kandy, the most powerful tribal ruler in the central part of the country. They also fought each other until 1656, when the Dutch defeated the Portuguese and came into sole control of Ceylon, a situation that lasted for the next 140 years.

The British arrived in 1782 and were able to take control of central Ceylon, promising to protect the Sinhalese king who maintained a shaky rule at Kandy. By 1815, they had abandoned their promises to the Sinhalese king, gained control of the entire country, and declared it a crown colony. The British quickly changed the economy in Ceylon from subsistence farming to a plantation system, and were immediately and impressively successful with planting coffee in the central mountains.

Any land owned by natives of Ceylon and wanted by the British was simply bought up by the crown. By 1835, four thousand acres had been planted in coffee. By 1845, the number of acres had increased to thirty-seven thousand. Just when it looked as if growth and profits were secure, the sheen began to come off the leaves—literally. Beginning in 1869, the leaves of coffee plants in some of the plantations began to show signs of a fungus. Within five years, the fungus had spread throughout the country, affecting every estate in Ceylon. By 1890, the export of coffee from Ceylon was less than a tenth of what it had been at its zenith, and it was simply not economically feasible to keep up production. Acres and acres of ruined coffee plantations lay fallow and were for sale for very little money.

Fortunately, many farmers had begun planting tea alongside coffee. When coffee could no longer be grown, many of the estates changed to planting tea. Many of the same problems encountered on Indian tea plantations were also seen in Ceylon, primarily a lack of robust seeds, seedlings, and expertise. In addition to this, there was serious economic hardship among the Sinhalese workers after the collapse of the coffee industry, but by 1900, three hundred eighty-four thousand acres were planted in tea, and it had become a major export crop for Ceylon. As in India, however, the majority of the plantations were owned by the British.

Many of the workers on Ceylon's tea plantations came from India, particularly after droughts in India caused famine, which happened in 1877. During this year, 167,000 Indian people of Tamil descent went to Ceylon to work. Many later returned to their homeland, but the net gain was tremendous for the plantations in Ceylon. Conditions on the plantations in Ceylon were no better than in India, although the pay was slightly higher. Child labor was still an accepted part of the labor agreement, and children began to work in the fields at the age of five, earning a few cents a day. The large numbers of immigrants of Tamil descent into Ceylon during the nineteenth century were resented by the native Sinhalese, which set the stage for the devastating ethnic conflicts that exist in Sri Lanka today.

The greatest landowner in Ceylon was Sir Thomas Lipton, who first became involved with tea production in Ceylon in 1890, and who eventually purchased three thousand acres in Ceylon for growing tea (see page 181).

Clipper Ships

The ships of the East India Company in the mid-nineteenth century were called "tea wagons." Big and solid, they were, literally, slow ships to China. After the company lost their China monopoly in 1834, they sold these ships (described as a cross between a medieval castle and a warehouse) to the merchants who had operated them under the rule of the East India Company, but they quickly became outdated, and sleeker and faster ships were built.

Once the monopoly was broken, all countries were able to trade at Canton. The United States and continental European countries began making the long, arduous but immensely profitable journey to China. Suddenly, speed became everything, for with the craze for tea in Great Britain, the first ships to dock in London, with the first supply of tea for the year, stood to make the highest profits for their goods.

It was clear to everyone that when it came to tea, time meant money, and the faster the ship, the greater the profit. The first tea crop of the year came from the Fujian region, where the major port was Foochow. After the Treaty of Nanking had opened this port up to British ships, it became the port of choice. Tea leaves picked and processed in Fujian in early spring were ready for loading on ships in Foochow in mid-June. The trip to take the tea from the remote tea gardens to the port took several weeks. Shanghai and Canton, which had a later harvest, did not have tea ready to load onto ships until five to six weeks later. This helped to make the first Fujian tea of the year a coveted and expensive commodity.

English tea drinkers grew obsessed with getting new tea from the first picking. It became prestigious to drink the first tea of the season—the "first flush" tea as it was called—and it was a mark of social status to acquire the freshest tea from the fastest ships. Pekoe from Fujian Province was one of the most expensive black teas to be picked and processed from the first crop in April. Of the first crop of green tea, "gunpowder," named for the distinctive round shape in which the leaves were rolled and dried, was most expensive. During the 1850s, black tea (such as pekoe) went primarily to England, and green tea was shipped to America.

And so the search was on for faster ships.

Showing the creativity and innovation that would mark them in the next century, Americans had developed fast sailing vessels called clipper ships during the War of 1812. The same speed that made them so successful during the war also made these sleek ships highly valuable for the tea trade. The first American clipper ship to carry tea from China to London was the *Oriental*, which made the journey from China to New York three times faster than the East India Company ships—in a mere ninety-seven days.

The first British clipper, the *Stornaway*, built in 1850, was patterned after an American ship captured during the War of 1812. A great rivalry grew between the American and British clipper ship builders and crew, although the Americans had to leave the competition when the American Civil War claimed their attention.

In England, however, increasing profits from trade with China took precedence over most other national concerns. Be-cause tea was such a valuable commodity and such an intimate part of social life throughout the country, there was much speculation about the arrival of the first tea of the year from Asia. As use of the clipper ships increased, and it was clear that the ships were becoming faster and faster, gambling on which ship would come into port first, and guessing the exact arrival time, engendered the enthusiasm usually reserved for a horse race. When the ships were due in, crowds gathered at the docks, waiting to see which ship would "win." The competition was more than sport, however, for the tea from the first ships in port commanded a much higher price per pound than that of later ships.

The glory of the age of the clipper ships hit its peak during the 1860s, and the most famous race was in 1866, when forty ships left China on the same day, and the first three ships arrived in London on the same tide. Two of the ships, *Ariel* and *Taeping*, finished in a dead heat in September 1866.

One of last clipper ships built was the *Cutty Sark*, launched in 1869. It was small and sleek but still carried a million pounds of tea.

The opening of the Suez Canal in 1869 and the advancement of steamships brought clipper ship races to an end, as steamships held the advantage over even the fastest sailing ships.

CHAPTER 9

Tea in England and the United States

> "It has a strange influence over mood, a strange power
> of changing the look of things, and changing it for the
> better, so that we can believe and hope and do under
> the influence of tea what we should otherwise give up
> in discouragement and despair."
>
> —The Lancet, *London, 1863*

TEA IN NINETEENTH-CENTURY ENGLAND

Half a globe and inconceivable differences separated the places where tea was grown and where tea was most enjoyed. While workers from Bengal were dying on the tea plantations in India, and coolies in China were struggling to bring three-hundred-pound loads of tea over steep mountain passes, tea was becoming a social phenomenon in England that eventually affected the lives of aristocrats and commoners alike.

Afternoon Tea

The idea of afternoon tea as a meal and a social event is universally attributed to Anna Maria Stanhope, Duchess of Bedford (1783–1857), wife of the seventh duke. She apparently often experienced what was commonly called "a sinking feeling" between lunch and the evening meal.

"There are few hours in life more
agreeable than the hour dedicated to
the ceremony known as afternoon tea."
—*Henry James (1843–1916)*

Thinking that a little sustenance might help, she began drinking tea and nibbling small savory treats in the late afternoon. In the first half of the nineteenth century, luncheon was a small meal taken during the middle of the day, and dinner was often not served until eight o'clock at night. The duchess found that taking tea with a little food in late afternoon was so beneficial and pleasant that she soon began inviting friends to join her at Belvoir Castle for this small afternoon meal, around five o'clock. The menu typically included small cakes, sandwiches of bread and butter, various sweets, and, of course, tea.

This practice had proven so successful and pleasant at her summer residence that when the family returned to London in the fall, Anna continued it, inviting friends for "tea and a walk in the fields" (fields were still plentiful close to London, in her day). The custom caught on with others, and soon many people copied her idea.

It was probably not until the middle of the nineteenth century that late-afternoon tea became an established custom throughout the country, and then, still only among the well-to-do. Queen Victoria loved tea, and her enthusiasm for the afternoon tea party made it even more popular. Afternoon tea receptions were introduced at Buckingham Palace in 1865.

High and Low Tea

With the growth in popularity of serving tea to friends and family, inevitably, a new set of rules also came into being. "Tea etiquette" became the rage, and new conventions and a new vocabulary quickly evolved.

There were many different kinds of meals and occasions that were called "tea." Today the terms "low tea" and "high tea" are often used incorrectly in the United States. A formal affair, "low tea" was called this because the tea and food were served on low tables next to armchairs on which the guests were seated. "High tea," on the other hand, indicated—and still does—a less formal, family affair served at 5:30 or 6:00, when workers returned from the field and children were home from school. High tea, also sometimes called "meat tea," was a much more substantial meal served on a kitchen or dining table, and included savory meats, soups, puddings and sweets, and lots of robust tea. High tea, then, referred *not* to "high society" but to the height of the table.

"At home tea" and "tea receptions" were huge social events that often included as many as two hundred guests. People customarily dropped by anytime between four and seven in the evening to enjoy bountiful displays of food and tea.

Tea for Everyone

In 1878, Samuel Phillips Day wrote in his book *Tea: Its Mystery and History*, of the working class family: "What was first regarded as a luxury, has now become, if not an absolute necessity, at least one of our accustomed daily wants. . . . Consumed by all classes, serving not simply as an article of diet, but as a refreshing, and invigorating beverage, tea cannot be too highly estimated."

By the time Queen Victoria died in 1901, tea was the drink for the masses in England. Tea's importance to the lower classes was exemplified by the women in small villages (particularly in Wales) who sometimes banded together to form "tea clubs." The purpose of these clubs was to get together in the afternoon and share tea, gossip, advice, and the like. When money was scarce, they shared responsibilities as well, one woman bringing the tea, another the biscuits or small breads, another bringing the teapot, and so forth.

Tea was served in the finest manor houses as well as the humblest cottage. Tea was served after lawn tennis, on picnics, after cycling—just about anywhere and everywhere that people gathered. Afternoon tea during the late nineteenth century and early twentieth century included many of the items that we traditionally associate with modern tea gatherings—scones or biscuits, éclairs, small cakes or muffins, small sandwiches, shortbreads, and larger cakes flavored with almond, ginger, or madeira.

How one drank tea soon became as important as when and with what. Ladies of high fashion thought that a teacup should be held with three fingers, with the pinky extended. This tradition went back to medieval times, when the gentry ate with three fingers, and commoners ate with five. An extended pinky finger became a mark of elitism and is still parodied as such today.

One custom that was *not* adopted by the British was the Chinese way of loudly slurping tea. The Chinese drank tea very hot, and it was perfectly acceptable (and even encouraged) to make loud slurping noises while drinking. The British disapproved.

The Temperance movement in England during the mid-nineteenth century provided an added incentive for drinking tea. At meetings throughout the country, tea was served as a replacement for gin or beer and was thought to be much healthier because it did not contain alcohol.

Tea Merchants

Not only international traders benefited from the wild popularity of tea, but domestic merchants as well. At the beginning of the nineteenth century, tea was still sold in bulk, but in 1826 a merchant by the name of John Horniman packaged and sold tea leaves in small boxes or tins. People loved this, particularly since Horniman guaranteed the quality of the product. Throughout the long history of tea in England, grocers who sold bulk tea were often tempted to add the dried leaves of other, less expensive plants to stretch out the costly Chinese tea. Prepackaged tea from a reputable merchant was a more dependable product, and Horniman's company prospered until it was finally bought out by Lyons in 1918.

As the nineteenth century progressed and tea was being produced in India and other places, several merchants

Thomas J. Lipton

began to specialize in tea. In England there were four major brands that dominated: Lyons, Brooke Bond, Ty-phoo (which produced just one blend and sold it at a single price, as a digestive aid), and the Co-op Wholesale Society in Manchester. The Co-op was established in 1863 and served as wholesaler to five hundred co-operative societies across Britain.

Of all the names associated with tea, Lipton is perhaps the best known. Sir Thomas Lipton was born in Glasgow in 1850 and worked in the family grocery store during his early years. When he was fifteen years old, he went to America and worked in the food section of a New York department store, where he fell in love with American advertising and merchandising. When he returned to Scotland, he opened his first small grocery store in Glasgow in 1871. By 1880, he owned and operated a chain of twenty general stores.

In 1890 Lipton went to Ceylon, where plant diseases had ruined the coffee plantations and land was selling cheaply.

Tea and War

Throughout the nineteenth century, tea continued to play a powerful role as an important commodity. By the end of the century, tea was an essential part of the daily rations of many armies throughout the world, including both British and American. It was considered necessary, not only because of its soothing effects, but perhaps more importantly, because tea necessitated boiling water, thus helping to ward off many of the intestinal diseases that had plagued armies for centuries.

Much has been written about the role tea played during the two world wars, not only as necessary refreshment for the troops but also as an item of trade. During the first two years of World War I, from 1914 to 1916, tea was enjoyed by the British as it had been before the war began. When German submarines began sinking British ships, however, supplies became less available, and the price of tea rose dramatically.

In response to the scarcity of tea, the government classified it as a luxury and began rationing it to civilians. The public uproar that resulted soon made it clear that tea would have to be reclassified as a basic necessity, essential for keeping up national morale. The government then took over all tea imports, fixed prices, and controlled sales. By 1918, all the tea available in Britain was owned and meted out by the government at the rate of two ounces of tea per week per person. In 1919, after the war ended, normal auctions resumed and consumption rose to three ounces of tea a head weekly by 1931.

While both world wars did have an impact on the world's consumption of tea, some things never change, and the British continued to import tea at an astronomic rate. Primarily through the efforts of the British-owned plantations, 470 million pounds of Indian tea were plucked in 1945, in spite of the turmoil in India during World War II. This was the largest tea crop ever from India, and British profits in tea increased by 200 percent.

Lipton bought four plantations and brought in ideas and innovations that quickly made him a very, very wealthy man. Although his estates in Ceylon could only supply a fraction of the tea he sold in a year, his advertising was so spectacular (his slogan was "Direct from the tea garden to the tea pot") that it seemed that everyone in the world soon knew of—and wanted—Ceylon tea.

By 1894, Lipton had a staff of five hundred working in London, and his employees in the plantations, offices, processing plants, and warehouses abroad numbered about ten thousand. Lipton's name became inseparably associated with tea and was known throughout the world.

TEA IN THE UNITED STATES

Tea in Colonial America

As the Dutch spread tea around the world during the seventeenth century, Peter Stuyvesant, Dutch governor in the American colonies, brought the first tea to New Amsterdam in 1647—interestingly enough, ten years before it was introduced to London. Early settlers quickly learned to love their tea. After New Amsterdam was captured by the English in 1674 and renamed New York, the British institutions of the coffeehouse and pleasure garden were brought to the New World.

In 1678, William Penn founded Philadelphia. His writings and diaries suggest that tea was his preferred drink. He wrote that cups filled with tea were "cups that cheer but not inebriate." By the 1690s, both "green and ordinary teas" were advertised in Boston newspapers. George Washington is known to have ordered six teapots and twelve pounds of tea, including the then popular hyson, in 1757.

The popularity of tea took on monumental importance,

A 1774 anti-tea political cartoon by Paul Revere: Tea being forced
down the throat of America

of course, as a symbol of the American Revolution. The tax
on tea that Parliament was imposing in its own country was
also applied to Americans, with disastrous results for the
British.

On December 16, 1773, a band of angry colonists gathered at Griffin's Wharf in Boston, disguised as native American Indians. They boarded three East Indian Company
ships and threw their tea cargoes into Boston Harbor, as a
protest against the unfair taxation.

These acts and others ultimately led to the Revolutionary War. For a while, drinking tea was seen as unpatriotic,
and citizens showed support by switching from tea to coffee
or other substitutes. Following the Boston Tea Party, young
ladies of Boston signed the following pledge:

> We the daughters of those patriots who have, and do
> now appear for the public interest, and in that princi-
> pally regard their posterity, as such do with pleasure
> engage with them in denying ourselves the drinking of
> foreign tea, in hopes to frustrate a plan that tends to
> deprive a whole community of all that is valuable to life.

After the war, people resumed drinking tea, and eventually the United States sent ships to China and began importing tea directly. Tea never became the national obsession in
America that it is in England—coffee seems to fill that role
in the U.S.—but the United States has been very involved
in the tea trade since the early nineteenth century.

The Merchant Princes of the New World

Three of America's first millionaires, T. H. Perkins of Boston, Stephen Girard of Philadelphia, and John Jacob Astor
of New York, earned fortunes from the China tea trade in

John Jacob Astor

the early nineteenth century. These entrepreneurs bought
tea directly from China and brought it to America, bypass-
ing the powerful East India Company.

John Jacob Astor, in particular, earned a massive fortune
through trade. He began in 1808 with the American Fur
Company, then bought five clipper ships and held a monopoly on the fur trade to China. He carried beaver and otter
pelts to China and returned with silk, tea, and tea ware. It
is said that part of his success lay in the fact that he made
up for the trade deficiency in gold, not opium, and that he
used the fastest ships available at the time. When the fur
trade began declining in 1810 and tea from India began to
cut into his China profits, Astor turned his attention to real
estate in New York, where he made even more money.

Tearooms

The turn of the last century in America saw a new rise in
popularity of tea that resulted in new "tearooms," or small
cafes that served tea and small snacks in the middle of the

afternoon. Many of these tearooms were found in department stores that first appeared during the 1890s. Taking tea after shopping became quite fashionable. In March 1908, *Harper's Bazaar* included a short piece about tearooms: "To-day, at the tea-hour smart carriages are drawn up in front of the tea-room; within, the merry tap of high heels on polished floors mingles with the fresh odor of violets and the rustle of many skirts. It is the fashion to drink tea in New York!"

It was the wealthy, of course, who could afford to go out in the middle of the day and visit tearooms. Tea, in a situation mirroring that in England, became an important element of the lives of the affluent. Soon teahouses, tearooms, and cafes sprang up around the countryside as well, particularly in areas frequented by tourists. This was a direct result of America's love affair with the automobile. Tea establishments proved to be wonderful destinations for the leisure class. Women, in particular, enjoyed the freedom of going out into the country, where small tearooms were very popular. These small cafes or restaurants served light meals and tea and provided refreshment for travelers. An article in *Good Housekeeping Magazine* in July 1917 said, "Until the automobile was graduated from the class of luxuries into that of necessities, tea-shops were successful only in the larger cities. Today they flourish in the smallest hamlets and flaunt their copper kettles and blue teapots on every broad highway."

In the early twentieth century, the best tearooms were found in fine hotels, which offered afternoon tea to guests

and patrons. One of most famous was the Palm Court at the Plaza Hotel in New York, which opened in 1907. This beautiful room was modeled after the winter garden in London's Hotel Carlton. Hotel tearooms often held enormously popular tea dances with a full orchestra, in the pre—World War I era.

Innovations

Americans were famous for their creative innovations at the turn of the century, and tea was not exempt from this fascination for making things new, easy, and somehow a little better. For example, the invention of the first tea bag is attributed to Thomas Sullivan of New York. Sullivan was a coffee and tea broker and, like others in the trade, he regularly sent samples of tea out to various merchants. In 1904, as a way of cutting costs, he decided to place single servings of loose tea in hand-sewn silk bags, rather than in small tin canisters, as was the custom of the day. The response was immediate and enthusiastic. People loved the ease of these little bags of tea—cleanup was so easy! Thomas Sullivan

"Meanwhile, let us have a sip of tea. The afternoon glow is brightening the bamboos, the fountains are bubbling with delight, the soughing of the pines is heard in our kettle. Let us dream of evanescence, and linger in the beautiful foolishness of things."

—*Kakuzo Okakura,*
The Book of Tea (*1906*)

realized he had hit on a gold mine of an idea and soon began manufacturing tea bags.

There were problems with these first tea bags, however—the most critical being the lack of space for the tea to expand, limiting the release of flavor. The solution was to use smaller leaves and pieces of tea, including fannings and dust, and for many years, tea made with tea bags was greatly inferior to the beverage derived from loose tea.

The situation was remedied, in part, in 1952, when the Lipton tea company developed a four-sided bag that they patented as "Flo-thru." Through the years, better bags have been developed, and a better grade of tea has been put into the bags, causing the tea bag to become more and more popular, not only in the United States but also in England. According to the U.K. Tea Council, in 2005, 96 percent of the tea sold in England was in the form of tea bags. There are still purists, however, who swear by loose tea and scorn the tea bag.

The United States has also been credited with "discovering" iced, sweetened tea. Although this innovation is often attributed to Richard Bloechynden, a vendor at the 1904 St. Louis World's Fair, cold, sweetened tea had actually been drunk in America for many years prior to that. To give Mr. Bloechynden credit, however, his serving of iced tea at the World's Fair did much to popularize and promote this new way of drinking tea.

According to Linda Stradley, cookbook author and regional foods expert, recipes for serving cold tea date back to the early nineteenth century, when both English and American cookbooks offered recipes for cold green tea punch—green tea served with copious amounts of alcohol. One of the first printed recipes for serving cold, sweetened black tea was found in *Mrs. Lincoln's Boston Cook Book: What to Do and What Not to Do in Cooking*, published in 1884. Mrs. Lincoln was the director of the Boston Cooking School, indicating that—contrary to popular belief—cold, sweet tea is not just a drink for Southerners.

Additional proof that iced tea predated the 1904 St. Louis World's Fair comes from a newspaper article in the *Nevada*

Noticer, dating to 1890. The article described a meeting of ex-Confederate veterans who gathered in Nevada, Missouri, for a huge picnic that included "11,000 pounds of beef—and 880 gallons of iced tea."

Tea Today in the U.S.A.

It used to be so simple to order a cup of tea! For decades, American tea choices were limited to bags of Lipton or Tetley, but today, there are an endless number of categories, types, blends, and brands of tea to choose from. America has grown to love the taste of tea. In 2005, the annual tea market in the United States was 6.8 billion dollars. This is expected to reach $10 billion by 2010.

Before World War II, 40 percent of all the tea drunk by Americans was green tea. The political climate during the war began to change this, however, when supplies of green tea from China and Japan were cut off, while supply lines from India and Ceylon remained open. Because India did—and still does—produce mostly black tea, Americans switched to drinking black. This trend has only recently begun to reverse again, as a result of much publicity over the health benefits of drinking green tea.

Although tea is definitely gaining in popularity in the United States, it only ranks sixth among the most-consumed beverages, after water, soft drinks, coffee, beer, and milk. The majority of the tea drunk by Americans (85 percent) is in the form of iced tea, in spite of great increases in drinking traditional teas. In 1995, South Carolina, home to the only commercially successful tea plantation in the

United States, declared tea their official "State Hospitality Beverage"—and a tall glass of iced tea is the hospitality they have in mind.

Americans have always been attracted to convenience, which is why tea bags caught on so quickly. Convenience has now taken another leap forward with the ready-to-drink bottled teas that are gaining tremendous popularity today. Americans never adopted the notion of stopping in the middle of the afternoon for a "cuppa." When it became possible, however, to grab a bottle or a can of tea and keep going, the American worker became more interested in the idea of drinking tea. Appealing to an increasingly health-conscious consumer, many major bottling companies have added both black and green tea or tea blends to the products they offer. Although the "goodies" found in tea, such as polyphenols and antioxidants, are greatly reduced in bottled tea, as compared to freshly brewed tea, these ready-to-drink teas are still much better for you than soft drinks.

Paralleling the situation in London in the late seventeenth and early eighteenth centuries, tea is also usually found at coffee shops. This trend began with chai, a blend of black tea, milk, and spices, and has continued to include a wide variety of teas, ranging from white to green to black and many different blends.

Tea's popularity can be witnessed in its increased presence in the media. From newspaper and magazine articles about the potential health benefits of tea to paid advertisements touting the delicious taste, tea seems to be everywhere, and the national awareness of tea is, undoubtedly, on the rise. Marketers use a "healthy lifestyle" approach today, capitalizing on the aura that sitting down with a cup of tea creates. Tea suggests something healthy and wholesome, something brand-new yet tinged with tradition, something slow and peaceful and mindful.

CHAPTER 10

Today and Tomorrow

"Drink your tea slowly and reverently, as if it is the
axis on which the world earth revolves—slowly,
evenly, without rushing toward the future."
—*Thich Nhat Hanh, Buddhist monk*

THE BUYERS AND SELLERS

According to a July 2005 report for the Food and Agriculture Organization of the United Nations, world tea production grew by 2 percent in 2004, reaching a record 3.2 million tons.

Who drinks all the tea produced? India still tops the list as the country that consumes the most—a total of 300,000 tonnes (330,690 U.S. tons) in 2004. Turkey ranks second at 180,000 tonnes (198,414 U.S. tons) for that year, followed by Russia with 171,000 tonnes (188,493 U.S. tons). Per capita statistics may be more meaningful, however. Turkey, as mentioned in the introduction to this book, has the highest rate of consumption per person per year (mostly black tea), followed by the United Kingdom and Morocco.

In spite of a recent decline, India still produced the greatest amount of tea at 820,000 tonnes (903,886 U.S. tons) in 2004, the last year for which full statistics are available. (Because Indians consume so much of their own tea, they are not the world's greatest *exporter* of tea; Kenya currently holds that position.) Second in production in 2004 was China, which is poised to increase production drastically in the next few years. Kenya was third in production in 2004 with 328,000 tonnes (361,554 U.S. tons), although persistent drought in 2005 allowed only a 1.2 percent increase in production—much lower than predicted. The drought is predicted to cause a sharp drop in production (anywhere from 16 percent according to the Kenya Tea Board to 25 percent according to other industry experts) in 2006. Sri Lanka produced 309,000 tonnes (340,612 U.S. tons) in 2004, and Turkey produced 205,000 tonnes (225,971 U.S. tons).

While worldwide tea production is up slightly and the popularity of tea in the United States and elsewhere is rising, the immediate outlook for the tea industry as a whole is not bright, because production is outpacing demand. In 1994, the World Trade Organization predicted that the worldwide production of tea would exceed demand by 1 percent by the year 2005. This did not happen, but possibly only because of the severe drought in Kenya, which had significant impact on world production.

Tea is grown in thirty-six tropical and subtropical countries. While newer tea-producing countries, such as Kenya, have been experiencing promising growth (unless hit by uncontrollable forces such as the 2005 drought), countries such as India, which have been producing tea for over a century, are experiencing declining productivity. The tea industry in India is in great need of restructuring, as old fields (some as old as 150 years) need replanting, the pro-

A tray for hand-picking
(after drawings by C. A. Bruce, 1838,
and J. C. Houssaye, 1843)

cessing plants need modernizing, and the welfare structure for workers is in desperate need of upgrading.

The greatest competition to these tea-producing countries is the quickly emerging power of China, which, before the beginning of the twenty-first century, had held only a minor position in the world production of tea for over one hundred years. According to a 2005 *New York Times* article, government subsidies in China helped increase tea exports by 18.9 percent in 2004, putting them on track to surpass both Kenya and Sri Lanka in the near future. Many of the Chinese state-owned tea farms operated inefficiently, but as these have been taken over by private entrepreneurs with a keen interest in the bottom line, production has increased remarkably. If China retakes the lead in the world production of tea, the country will come full circle with regard to its place in the history of tea.

Ironically, though, the Chinese themselves are drinking less tea than they ever have before. After thousands of years of revering tea, the Chinese have recently developed a taste for coffee and sodas, and domestic consumption of tea is down—meaning that there is plenty of tea to export. These circumstances have experts throughout the world concerned about a flood of Chinese tea in the world market, a

"Given a person in good health
and without any individual nervous
peculiarity . . . and the moderate
drinking of tea, coffee, and cocoa
is not harmful. Much that is said
on this point is claptrap, and
promulgated often for a strictly
selfish commercial end."
—*G. F. Lydston, M.D., Chicago,*
in the New York Herald, *Dec. 2, 1905*

situation that is particularly worrisome to developing countries that depend heavily on the tea industry. Indonesia,
India, and Sri Lanka (where 10 percent of the population
depends on income generated by the tea industry) are especially vulnerable to competition from China.

THE WORKERS

Tea is a very labor-intensive crop to grow. Although
machines are used for picking the leaves at many plantations, almost all of the highest-quality tea is still picked
by hand, just as it was in China almost two thousand years
ago—meaning that most tea planters still require a large
labor force. Women constitute a large part of this work
force.

Plucking takes accuracy, as only the top leaves and bud
are picked for the finest teas. A good tea plucker must also
be fast to fill her daily quota. An experienced plucker per-
forms the picking motion approximately fifty thousand

Wanajasa Tea Plantation and Factory about 1836; after a sketch by Jacobson

times a day, and usually harvests at least 54 kilograms (119 pounds) per day. The leaves are picked with the thumb and forefinger, then tossed into a basket carried on the plucker's back. The basket is the only receptacle for the leaves, meaning that the worker must carry the full weight on her back. The repetitive work is boring, the conditions are often difficult, and the hours are long. Piya Chatterjee, author of *A Time for Tea: Women, Labor, and Post/Colonial Politics on an Indian Plantation*, lived on tea plantation in Dooars, India, for several seasons. She writes about women laborers during the 1990 plucking season, who left their homes at 6:00 a.m., plucked until 11:00 a.m., then walked two miles to a checkpoint, carrying full baskets of leaves that weighed between 30–35 kilograms (66–77 pounds). After a short break while the leaves were being weighed and checked, they walked back to the fields for an afternoon of picking.

Even though the work is difficult and the hours are long, those people in India who still have a job in the tea plantations feel fortunate, for many of the plantations have been forced to close, resulting in devastating conditions for workers.

The Indian tea industry has been in crisis for several years, a situation due to a combination of factors. In addition to aging plants and outdated processing machinery, the demand for Indian tea has sharply decreased. For many years, the USSR provided a secure market for Indian tea, but with the fall of the Soviet Union, this ready market disappeared. Another determining factor in the decreasing demand is the liberal globalization policies of the Indian government, which have allowed cheap tea from Kenya and other countries to flood the market. The third major factor is the weather (primarily drought), which has been devastating for the tea plants during the past several years, resulting in decreased productivity. The combination of all these factors has forced many tea plantations to close, at least temporarily, leading to a humanitarian crisis among the tea workers of India, particularly on plantations in West Bengal, Assam, Tamil Nadu, and Kerala.

Because tea farms operate under a plantation system, whereby workers are completely dependent on the plantation for housing, food, schooling, medicine, and the like, when a plantation shuts down, there is nowhere for the workers and their families to go. The crisis in this region of

"Tea and coffee drinking cause much less injury than over-eating—an important thing to consider in these days when young and old are desirous of a svelte appearance, and when over-eating is the commonest vice of each group."

—*Hugh A. McGuigan,*
Pharmacologist,
B.S., Ph.D., M.D., Chicago;
Tea and Coffee Trade Journal,
New York, April 1930

India alone affects over one hundred thousand workers. On the closed and abandoned plantations, workers are now subsisting at below-poverty level. There is dilapidated housing; rampant disease, including AIDS; no medicines; no schooling for young children, and no transportation to school for older children; a critical lack of clean drinking water; and, perhaps most devastating of all, insufficient food. The International Union of Food, Agricultural, Hotel, Restaurant, Catering, Tobacco and Allied Workers' Associations (IUF) reported in 2006 that "thousands of workers have starved to death since then [2001] despite attempts to get them food aid and other assistance."

In many cases, the plantation owners have absconded with worker pension funds that have been valued at as much as seventeen months' worth of worker wages. There have been pleas to the Indian government to help in this crisis. The Plantation Labor Act of 1951 established laws protecting the workers, but these have not been enforced. The government has provided some relief, but starvation and a lack of medicine and clean drinking water continue to be critical.

India is not the only country that faces challenges in bringing humanitarian aid and rights to these workers. Some of the gravest issues include child labor, exploitation of women, and the rampant spread of HIV and AIDS. In addition, increased mechanization among the larger tea growers poses the threat of lost jobs. Machines are not as selective or as careful as human hands, but they can pick, at the minimum, twenty times more tea per day than a human worker. The lure of bigger profits is still as appealing to tea plantation owners as in the past.

In all areas where tea is grown, workers and small growers are facing disturbing challenges brought on by globalization and open trading borders. These policies, backed by the World Trade Organization (WTO), benefit the big tea brands at the expense of the workers and independent growers. In 2005, an International Tea Conference composed of tea workers and small growers from eleven tea-producing countries from Africa, South Asia, and East Asia met to draw up specific provisions to protect these groups. This conference declared

A tea catalog (1841)

December 15, 2005, and the same day every year thereafter, to be International Tea Day—a time to draw attention to the impact that the tea trade has on laborers, small growers, and consumers.

RESPONSIBLE CONSUMERISM

For Westerners, tea has always suggested refinement, sophistication, and elegance. Today, tea also offers a calming and healthy influence—an antidote for the hectic lives we live. But, as has happened throughout history, the cost to others when we purchase such commodities is much steeper than the price we pay for them. In the case of tea, however, there are ways that consumers can make ethical and responsible purchases—and still buy as much tea as they desire.

The Fair Trade Organization offers a certification program that helps family farmers in developing countries get direct access to international markets and receive fair prices for their products. The goal is to provide for a better life for farmers and workers. Tea is one of the fastest-growing Fair Trade Certification product categories. As of September 2006, Fair Trade certificates were awarded to seventy tea estates and small-scale producers in eleven countries in Asia, Africa, and Latin America. Most Fair Trade certificate recipients are also certified organic, making their products a good purchase on all accounts, except perhaps financially. As expected, Fair Trade products are generally more expensive than those that are not certified because most Fair Trade—certified producers do not benefit from the same economies of scale as larger companies, and because they offer workers fair wages. For a complete listing of the brands that have received Fair Trade Certification, go to the Transfair Web site at www.transfairusa.org.

Another industry watchdog is the Ethical Tea Partnership, which monitors living and working conditions on tea estates to ensure that participating members produce tea in a socially responsible way. Tea estates from eleven different countries are members of this partnership and produce popular brands.

TEA-GROWING COUNTRIES

CHINA

China's tea production is legendary—literally. There are rumors and stories of China's sacred gardens, which—for hundreds, if not thousands, of years—produced teas just for the emperor and his court. Today, special teas are grown and produced just for the highest-ranking party officials. No visitors are allowed in these most sacred gardens, and nothing is permitted that might compromise the purity of the tea. Some of the legendary teas produced in such gardens include Pei Hou, a green tea purported to grow in a tea garden only reached by a five-hour trek.

Whether the leaves are picked by virgins in white gloves or by workers toiling in the vast tea gardens in China, this country of tea's origin still produces some of the finest teas in the world. China produces green, white, oolong, and black teas of excellent quality. Black tea is often called "red tea" in China.

Tea is grown in eighteen regions in China. The five main provinces are Zhejiang, Hunan, Szechwan, Fujian, and Anhui. The first crop is picked, or plucked, from mid-April to mid-May and constitutes over 50 percent of the total harvest for the year. A second harvest is done in early summer, and in some regions, a third harvest is done in early autumn.

TAIWAN (FORMOSA)

Taiwan was known as Formosa (a word that means "beautiful") under Japanese rule and has retained this name to refer to various excellent teas produced on the island. Although it has been claimed that the first tea produced on Taiwan was made from wild plants, in the 1860s tea was already being cultivated there and became an important export. The first teas produced were oolong, and this remains, today, the primary type of tea exported from Taiwan.

Taiwan has a subtropical climate but boasts tall mountains. This combination of climate and geography is excellent for growing tea bushes.

INDIA

India now produces primarily black teas, characterized by a full body and rich taste. Indian teas vary from one district to another, as with different wine-producing regions. Each region produces tea with distinctive and unique flavors.

Darjeeling. Darjeeling tea plantations are found on the southern slopes of the Himalayas in northeastern India. The average elevation in this important tea-growing region is 2,134 meters (6,982 feet). Considered the champagne of tea, these teas are generally the highest grade available. Differences in Darjeeling teas come more from the harvest season than from individual gardens or plantations.

Assam. This region is found in northern India on a high plateau that straddles the Brahmaputra River. It is the largest tea-growing region in the world. The first flush is harvested beginning in February, although it is the second flush, harvested in May and June, that makes the finest teas. Assam produces full-bodied teas, good with milk. Assam teas are often used in blends.

Nilgiri. This region is found in southern India on the hilly uplands. The main provinces include Kerala, Tamil Nadu, and Karnataka. Nilgiri produces light, delicate teas, primarily used in blends.

JAPAN

The largest tea-growing region in Japan is Shizuoka, at the foot of Mt. Fuji. Over half the tea produced in Japan comes from this one region. Other tea-producing regions include Kagoshima, on the island of Kyushu, and the Uji district of Kyoto. Japan produces primarily green tea but offers a large variety of kinds.

SRI LANKA (CEYLON)

Tea from Sri Lanka has traditionally been called Ceylon, after the old name for the island, but in 2006, the government of Sri Lanka decided to change this tradition and use the modern name of the country for its teas. Known as the "Isle of Tea," Sri Lanka has six major production regions: Dimbula, Galle, Kandy, Nuwara Eliya, Ratnapura, and Uva, each producing tea with a distinctive flavor. (For a history of the tea industry in Sri Lanka, see pages 169–171.)

Today, Sri Lanka produces mostly black teas that differ in taste according to the elevation at which they grow. These can be divided into three categories: Lower-growing varieties below 650 meters (2,132 feet) have a dark, strong taste and are primarily used in blends. Middle regions, between 650 and 1,300 meters (2,132–4,265 feet) and higher regions, between 1,300 and 2,500 meters (4,265–8,202 feet) produce the best quality of tea.

INDONESIA

Tea has been grown in Indonesia since the Dutch brought Chinese plants to the islands in the 1700s. Initial attempts were not very successful, but eventually the plantations began to show much more promise when assam plants were used in place of the sinensis variety. The Indonesian tea industry was almost completely annihilated during World War II, when tea plantations experienced tremendous damage. Plants were flattened or broken or, at best, neglected. It wasn't until 1984 that Indonesia made a significant comeback under the auspices of the Tea Board of Indonesia.

Most of the tea grown in Indonesia today is processed as black tea used for blending, and most of it is grown on the island of Java. Although it is harvested year-round, the best quality is picked during the dry season of August and September.

EAST AFRICA

Kenya produces the most tea of any country in Africa (and recently, more than any other country in the world). Tea was introduced by the British in 1903, but at first only on a limited scale. Two British companies, Brooke Bond and James Finlay, changed this in the 1920s, when they were able to purchase massive amounts of land very cheaply, although with some controversy. Land in Kenya was made available to British ex-servicemen after World War I, a fact that was naturally greatly resented by the African landowners. Twenty-five thousand acres had been set aside for growing flax, a scheme engineered by fifty-five British ex-officers. Unfortunately, the flax market collapsed, and the entire enterprise fell apart. The land was put on the market for almost nothing and was quickly snatched up by the companies James Finlay (now called African Highlands) and Brooke Bond (now part of Unilever), which were both determined to grow tea there. This part of Kenya proved to be excellent for growing tea. Other British companies began buying and planting land in Kenya as well, until 1976, when the Kenyan government finally was able to stop further expansion of the British tea industry. As of the year 2000, the British companies had planted over fifty thousand acres of tea. Brooke Bond was the biggest owner.

In 1976, the Kenya Tea Development Authority Insurance Agency was founded. This organization, funded by the World Bank, encouraged individual African landowners to grow tea. Although each landowner only planted a small amount, usually only about one acre, so many farmers became involved in the project that small landholders now account for 60 percent of the tea produced in Kenya. June 2000 brought change to this group, as it switched from being a parastatal agency (one wholly or partially owned by the government) to a public company. The name was changed to the Kenya Tea Development Agency.

The highest-quality tea produced in Kenya tastes somewhat like assam tea. Leaves are harvested during the driest months, August and September. Most Kenyan tea is low quality, used in blends and tea bags.

SOUTH AMERICA

The United States is a very large importer of tea from Argentina, which produces low- to medium-quality, inexpensive tea used in instant tea, tea blends, and tea bags. The Argentinian plantations are generally found in the northern part of the country in a region called Missiones. For the most part, the leaves are harvested mechanically, resulting in a less-expensive, lower-quality product. Argentina teas are medium body, earthy tasting, with a dark, rich color.

THE UNITED STATES

Tea plants were first introduced to America in 1799 by André Michaux, a French botanist who brought many beautiful and exotic plants to this country. Tea was planted at the Middleton Barony near Charleston, South Carolina (now open as a public garden known as Middleton Place), and by the middle of the nineteenth century, it was grown in many places in the state. Several attempts were made at growing tea commercially, but all failed, more from human mishaps and accidents than for horticultural reasons.

One attempt was made by Dr. Charles Shepard, who founded the Pinehurst Tea Plantation in Summerville, South Carolina, in 1888. This plantation declined after Shepard's death in 1915. In 1968, the Thomas J. Lipton

Company established an experimental tea farm, testing the possibilities of growing tea on Wadmalaw Island in South Carolina, and found that tea could indeed be grown successfully along this Southern coast. In 1987, Mack Fleming, a manager at Lipton, and his partner, Bill Hall (a third-generation tea producer), purchased the research farm and established the Charleston Tea Plantation. Their product, American Classic Tea is, so far, the only tea ever produced commercially in America. The Charleston Tea Plantation opened for public tours in January 2006.

THE PROFESSIONALS' TERMS
FOR DESCRIBING TEA

Like terms for describing wine, those for revealing the subtle flavors and nuances of tea may be a little vague until you have a lot of tea-tasting experience.

TERMS FOR DESCRIBING BREWED TEA

Aroma. This term refers to the way brewed tea smells.

Body. How the liquid feels on the tongue. This could be wispy, light, medium, or full. A full-bodied black tea such as Keemun lingers on the tongue, while a delicate white such as Silver Needles is wispy, seeming to evaporate immediately.

Brassy. A strong taste, usually a little bitter. This happens when leaves for processing black tea have not been withered long enough.

Brisk. Pleasing, slightly tangy.

Burnt. Burnt tea tastes a little like burnt toast. Caused by overfiring, this is not a desirable characteristic.

Coarse. Coarse tea has a decidedly acidic taste, also a little bitter.

Crisp. Disappears quickly on the tongue; a desirable quality.

Earthy. An earthy taste is a little moldy, which may be caused by improper firing.

Flowery. Flowery tea has a hint of floral sweetness, like chamomile.

Malty. A malty flavor tastes like steamed green vegetables, with a touch of honey and citrus—a desirable characteristic.

Mellow. Mellow tea is smooth and pleasant on the palate.

Muscatel. Tastes like the Muscat grape. This term is often associated with Darjeeling teas.

Smoky. A smoky flavor has a touch of smoke or tar. Lapsang souchong, for example, is made by burning pine logs and branches to create the heat for the drying process, giving the tea a distinctive smoky taste.

Sweet. A sweet taste is a pleasant, often smooth and fruity, flavor.

Vegetal. A desirable characteristic for green teas, a vegetal taste is grassy or similar to steamed asparagus.

TERMS FOR DESCRIBING THE DRY LEAF

Brown. This is an undesirable color for any tea leaf, including black tea.

Chunky. This is a favorable term, describing large tip pieces.

Golden tip. A great feature for teas, golden tip tea produces an amber-colored brew.

Neat. Neat tea leaves are well made and attractive.

Stalky. This term indicates that pieces of undesirable stalk were included with the leaves.

Stylish. A very favorable characteristic; stylish leaves are especially neat and attractive.

CHOICE TEAS
FROM AROUND THE WORLD

Although tea is grown all over the world, the best-grade teas are thought to grow in only five countries, Sri Lanka, China, Taiwan, India, and Japan. Countries such as Kenya and Argentina generally produce a low- to medium-quality tea that is used in blends, tea bags or instant powdered tea.

The "best" teas are, of course, a matter of taste and may depend on such vague and esoteric factors as one's mood or the time of day. The following are just general descriptions of a few teas that are readily available. The best way to find a favorite tea is to drink a lot of different kinds—and keep notes. Happy sipping!

BLACK TEAS

Milk is a good addition to some black teas. See notations below: *w* (with) or *wo* (without) milk.

Assam (India). Robust, full-bodied, used in blends, malty [*w milk*]

Ceylon (Sri Lanka). Crisp, light to medium body, sweet [*w or wo milk*]

Darjeeling, first flush (India). Sweet Muscat, crisp [*w or wo milk*]

Dian hong (Yunnan, China). Rich, spicy, smooth [*wo milk*]

Keemun (China). Deep, rich, hint of smoke [*wo milk*]

Kenilworth (Ceylon). Brisk, strong [*w milk*]

Lapsang souchong. Smoky, full-bodied [*w or wo milk*]

Nilgiri (India). Smooth, full-bodied, hint of sweet, blends [*wo milk*]

Sikkim (north of Darjeeling). Fruity, sweet [*wo milk*]

GREEN TEAS

Bancha (Japan). Good "everyday" tea, light golden color, slightly sweet, grassy

Dragonwell, or Longjing (China, Japan). Very fine, bright, brisk, sweet

Gunpowder (China, Japan, Ceylon). Named for its pellet shape; strong body, sweet, grassy

Genmaicha (Japan). Blended with roasted brown rice; popcorn taste

Gyokuro (Japan). Very fine, light green brew; sweet, taste of the sea

Hojicha (Japan). From toasted leaves, amber brew, nutty taste, full-bodied

Hyson (China). Earthy, medium body

Matcha (Japan). A ceremonial tea, ground into powder; light, sweet

Sencha (Japan). Nice "everyday" tea, slightly astringent, slightly sweet

OOLONG TEAS

Formosa (Taiwan). Smooth, medium body, fruity

Imperial (Taiwan). Very fine, slight honey taste, amber, mild

Ti Kuan-yin, Iron Goddess of Mercy (Taiwan, China). Mild, good for digestion

Tung ting jade (Taiwan). Smooth, flowery

WHITE TEAS

Silver Needles, *yin zhen* (Fujian, China). Light, slightly vegetal, exotic and expensive

White Peony (China). Light, clear brew, slightly grassy

BLENDS

The majority of teas available on the market today are blends of different kinds of teas from different growing regions. For example, "English breakfast" tea is made up of a blend of black teas from Nilgiri and Ceylon. Irish breakfast tea, which is a little stronger with a bolder flavor, is composed of black teas from Nilgiri, China, and Assam.

Teas are also blended with any number of flavorings from fruits and flowers. Earl Grey is a black China tea flavored with oil of bergamot. Favorite flavorings come from jasmine, peach, orange, lemon, hibiscus, bergamot, cinnamon, vanilla, and almond.

LESS WELL KNOWN TYPES OF TEA

Pu-erh

One of the most unusual of all teas is the ancient Pu-erh of Yunnan, China. Some experts date the production of

Pu-erh back to the Eastern Han Dynasty (25–220 CE). Unlike other kinds of tea, Pu-erh is traditionally made from large, older leaves that measure longer and wider than a human hand. Yunnan, one of the earliest tea-producing regions of China, is one of the few places—if not the only place—where older trees exist that can produce such leaves. These leaves are covered with fine hair and have a different chemical composition than the younger leaves.

Pu-erh is a "living" tea that, like yogurt, includes many microbes and continues to change and evolve as it ages. These microbes are thought to have tremendous health benefits, including lowering cholesterol and aiding digestion.

There are two basic types or categories of Pu-erh tea: green and cooked. Green Pu-erh tea is allowed to age naturally. The leaves are pressed into cakes or bricks, wrapped in paper or bamboo, and left to age for several years. Enough moisture is left in the leaves for the tea to continue to ferment slowly over a very long time. The bricks are then stored underground for several years to age to perfection. The entire process can take as long as thirty years. The second type of Pu-erh tea is cooked to speed the aging time. Most cooked Pu-erh teas peak at about fifteen years.

Pu-erh is the only tea that actually improves with age. In the West, most Pu-erh is served in restaurants, and the quality is often inferior. A good Pu-erh tea has a clean and flowery taste.

Iron Goddess of Mercy

One of the best oolong teas available is Iron Goddess of Mercy. This was originally produced in China's Fujian Province, although it is now grown on Taiwan as well. A legend says that long ago there was a tea grower in this part of China known as Mr. Wei. Every day, on his way to tend to the tea plants, Mr. Wei passed a temple dedicated to Kuan-yin, goddess of mercy. After years of neglect, the temple was in a dilapidated condition, a situation that so saddened Mr. Wei that, every month, on the first and the fifteenth, he would stop and burn incense at the temple, and he worked to keep it as clean as possible.

One night Kuan-yin appeared to him in a dream and told him that in the cave behind the temple he would find a treasure that would last generations—but that he had to share it generously. Mr. Wei ran to the cave, but all he found was a small tea plant. Disappointed, he nevertheless put it in his garden and tended it. In two years, it yielded a catty (about 1.3 pounds) of tea. He brewed some of this and found it to have a pure, strong flavor and an unusual fragrance. In a few years, this plant had produced two hundred offspring. When Mr. Wei began to sell the tea, he called it Ti Kuan-yin, Iron Goddess of Mercy, after the iron statue of Kuan-yin at the temple.

Chai

Chai is the Indian word for tea, but today the term indicates a sweet concoction made from black tea, milk, sugar, and spices. Chai spices include cardamom, cinnamon, ginger, black pepper, clove, Indian bay leaf, and nutmeg.

Bubble Tea

The latest tea fad began in Taiwan during the 1980s, when tea vendors outside a school began adding black tapioca "pearls" and various sweet flavorings to cold, infused tea. This concoction is shaken, and the pearls settle to the bottom of the glass and look like bubbles. Other names for bubble tea include pearl tea drink, boba drink, and several other variations of these names. Tapioca pearls are made from the root of cassava mixed with brown sugar or caramel. They are about the size of a small marble and have the consistency of a gummy worm or other gummy or soft candy.

Bubble tea is enormously popular in Taiwan, Hong Kong, and other places in Southeast Asia, and continues to gain popularity in the United States.

Sherpa

This is a blend of oolong and Darjeeling teas that tastes delicious even with lower water temperatures. This makes it great for brewing at high elevations—such as the Himalayan home of the Sherpa people—where it is difficult to get water to boil.

TISANES, OR HERBAL "TEAS"

All tea is made from *Camellia sinensis*, but there are many, many other infusions that are called "teas," although they are made from other plants and are more correctly termed "tisanes." Two of the most popular of these are *rooibos* from South Africa and *yerba maté* from South America, but numerous herbal teas are made from plants throughout the world. They have widely varying health benefits, from none at all to substantial.

Please note that it's essential to be careful when using or ingesting any plant foods or drinks. Consult a physician before deciding whether an infusion or a tisane is safe for you.

ROOIBOS

Red tea, red bush tea, or rooibos (pronounced roy-boss) is made from the leaves of a plant native to South Africa, *Aspalathus linearis*. Only introduced to the West relatively recently, it has been known to the people of the Cedarberg Mountain region of South Africa for about three hundred years. Indigenous people collected branches of leaves and stems, then hammered or bruised them to release moisture. They then stacked the cut branches in the sun to ferment or oxidize. ("Green" red tea is also available. This undergoes a processing similar to that of green tea, with a limited oxidation process.) Once they are dry, the leaves are placed in boiling water to make a tea (tisane) that is remarkably sweet and full of antioxidants.

Health claims for rooibos began in 1968, when a young mother gave her colicky baby a tea made from this plant and found that it immediately soothed the child. She spread the word, and the results are proving to be quite encouraging. The tea is said to be soothing and healthful, although these claims have not been substantiated through formal testing. In addition, it is known that rooibos is high in antioxidants—less than in green tea, but more than in black tea, and it has no caffeine, so it can be consumed in larger quantities without side effects.

Rooibos is often blended with other flavorings such as raspberry, hibiscus, almond, and vanilla.

YERBA MATÉ

This strongly flavored tisane is made from the dried leaves of *Ilex paraguariensis*, which grows in many places in South America. It has been used for centuries by the natives, who found that it helped them resist fatigue and made them less susceptible to the effects of thirst and hunger.

Traditionally, yerba maté is poured into a hollowed calabash (gourd) and drunk through a straw, which helps filter out large bits of leaves. The brew tastes like both green tea and coffee, with additional hints of tobacco smoke. There is an ongoing argument about whether yerba maté contains mateine or caffeine, and what the difference is between the two. Whatever you call it, the substance within yerba maté produces the same stimulating effects as the caffeine found in coffee and tea.

HOMEMADE TISANES

Apple. Although "apple tea" more often than not is made up of apple flavoring in black tea, it's also possible to make a tisane from dried apples and flowers, creating a fruity, caffeine-free drink. Add equal amounts of dried apple, hibiscus flowers, chamomile, and dried cranberries. Place in boiling water and brew for five to seven minutes. Sweeten with honey, if desired.

Basil. Use two tablespoons of fresh basil leaves. There are many different kinds of basils available. Try either the common variety or cinnamon, lemon, or spicy basil. Place them in a nonreactive pot and add one cup of boiling water; brew for five to six minutes. This makes a spicy tea good for keeping one alert. It is also sometimes used to combat the effects of motion sickness.

Blackberry. Pick one handful of green leaves and place them in a saucepan. Add two cups of water and simmer for ten minutes. Strain into cups and sweeten with honey. This was used by southern Appalachian folk healers to treat diarrhea and as a blood purifier and tonic.

Blueberry. Use one handful of fresh leaves or about one tablespoon of dried leaves per two cups of water. Boil for about five minutes, then strain and sweeten. Blueberries are native to North America, and Native American healers used blueberry tea to prevent the formation of kidney or bladder stones and to treat diarrhea and problems with the kidneys, as it helps to increase the flow of urine. The cooled tea was gargled to treat mouth sores. The best and most flavorful leaves are those picked in early spring.

Borage. To make the tisane, take two tablespoons of fresh leaves and/or chopped stems, add one cup of boiling water, and steep for about five minutes. Borage tea was drunk by the ancient Romans to treat depression and as a diuretic, demulcent, and emollient. Applied externally, the tisane was used for inflammations and swelling. Borage tea, like tea made from *Camellia sinensis*, is high in tannins and is slightly astringent. It has a mild cucumber flavor and is high in calcium and potassium.

Catnip. Use one tablespoon of dried leaves and flowers (or two tablespoons of fresh leaves) to every cup of boiling water. Allow to steep for three to five minutes. Catnip tea has enjoyed a wide variety of uses, but is perhaps best known as a digestive aid. It is also a very, very mild sedative and is good for drinking before going to bed. The most effective elements are found in the plant's volatile oils, so the tisane should be covered while brewing, to prevent them from being lost.

Chamomile. Use one tablespoon of dried buds or flowers for every cup of boiling water. Steep for three to five minutes, then strain and sweeten, if desired. Chamomile has been beloved as a medicine in Europe for many centuries. The flowers contain a volatile oil that has been, and still is, used as an anti-inflammatory (for skin disorders such as acne and eczema), an antispasmodic (for indigestion and menstrual cramps), and an anti-infective for minor infections. Its flowery, sweet taste makes it a popular tea. The tea is made from the flowers and contains pollen. For this reason, people with an allergic reaction to ragweed and other flowering plants should use caution when taking this tisane.

Chicory. The roasted root makes a very bitter, dark brew, more like coffee than tea. Boil one tablespoon of the root with one cup of water for three to four minutes, and strain into a cup. This tisane has been used medicinally in Europe since the first century CE. It has been grown in the United States since Thomas Jefferson planted it at Monticello. It has now escaped from cultivation and grows wild throughout many parts of the country. The ancient Greeks used it as a mild tonic and laxative.

Elderberry. Place one tablespoon of dried elderberry flowers in a ceramic teapot and add one cup of boiling water. Steep for three to five minutes, then strain. Take care when ingesting elderberry, as the roots, stems, and leaves are slightly toxic. The ripe berries and flowers, however, are not only nontoxic, they are delicious in things such as tisanes, jelly, and pie. A tisane made from the flowers has traditionally been used as a stimulant and as a diaphoretic to induce sweating. The Shakers used the elderberry to treat migraine headaches.

Ginger. To make a ginger tisane, pour two cups of boiling water over about one ounce of chopped ginger root, and allow to steep for fifteen to twenty minutes. The tisane is used to treat indigestion, flatulence, and motion sickness. It was exported from its native Asia to Greece as early as 2000 BCE.

Ginseng. To make a tisane, take five to eight small slices from the ginseng root or one teaspoon of the dried, ground root, and add one cup of boiling water. Steep for five to six minutes, strain, and sweeten to taste. Ginseng has been revered as a powerful healing herb for over two thousand years, particularly in China. It was thought not only to prolong life but also to cure an enormous number of ailments—and to be effective as an aphrodisiac. It is one of the most used and most touted of all folk medicines.

Hibiscus. Place one tablespoon of dried hibiscus flowers in a teapot and add one cup of boiling water. Allow to steep for three to five minutes, then strain into a cup to make a sweet, fruity beverage. The flowers are slightly astringent, while the roots are mucilaginous. Hibiscus flowers are often added to other herbal teas and to flavored black tea and rooibos tisane.

Lemon balm (also known as Melissa, from *Melissa officinalis*). Use one handful of fresh green leaves, add two cups of boiling water, and steep for seven to nine minutes. Strain and sweeten with honey. Tisane made from lemon balm is very soothing. It has also been used against bacteria and viruses. The fresh leaves, rubbed on the skin, can bring instant relief to irritation from insect bites.

Licorice. The tisane cannot be made from fresh roots. The roots need to be shade-dried for about six months, then ground into a powder for using. Pour boiling water over powder, and stir to dissolve. Licorice tisane has a long and rich history. It was used in Europe to treat infections, canker sores, colic, hepatitis, and epilepsy. In traditional Chinese medicine, it is used as a demulcent to treat digestive and urinary disorders, as well as coughs and sore throats. It is an anti-inflammatory, and the tisane is often taken to relieve pain from arthritis.

Linden. The tisane is made from the pale yellow flowers that occur in summer. Use one tablespoon of flowers per cup of boiling water. Allow it to steep for three to five minutes, then strain. Linden tisane was known in ancient

Europe as the "royal nectar" because it was used for so many things, including improving circulation, relieving tension, and aiding digestion.

Mint. Pick a handful of green leaves. Pour one cup of boiling water over the leaves and steep for six to eight minutes, then strain. Mint is probably the best-known and most widely used herb for making tisanes. Its refreshing, sweet flavor has made it a favorite for hundreds of years. There are numerous kinds of mint, including peppermint and spearmint. Mint tea, almost all experts agree, helps in treating indigestion, flatulence, and colic. It's also used effectively to treat muscle spasms and menstrual cramps, and is used externally on insect bites and chapped skin. Mint tea can be made by pouring boiling water over either fresh or dried leaves.

Passionflower. To make a tisane, add one-half to one teaspoon of the dried flowers to a cup of boiling water, steep for three to five minutes, and strain. A tisane made from the beautiful, exotic-looking flowers has a slightly narcotic effect, and has been used to treat insomnia, muscle spasms, and tension. Native American healers rubbed the crushed leaves on the skin to treat bruises.

Raspberry. Place one handful of the green leaves in a saucepan. Add two cups of water and simmer for ten minutes, strain, and sweeten with honey. In Colonial America, raspberry tisane was used to treat diarrhea in children, and as a gargle and mouthwash to fight against infection and disease. Raspberry-leaf tea was given to expectant mothers to tone the uterine and pelvic muscles. In Chinese medicine, raspberries and raspberry-leaf tisane are used to strengthen the kidneys.

Rose. Place four to six dried rose hips in a nonaluminum saucepan. Add two cups of cool water. Simmer for about twenty to thirty minutes. Strain and sweeten with honey. Rose hip tea has been used to cure a wide variety of ailments, including toothaches and earaches; diseases of the stomach, lungs, and intestines; overindulgence in wine; headaches; hemorrhages; sleeplessness; excessive perspiration; and hydrophobia. Rose hips are extremely high in vitamin C (more so than oranges), and in vitamins A, B, and E. Rose hip tea is slightly astringent.

APPENDIX E

TEA WITH FOOD

Different teas taste best with different kinds of food. As with wine, much depends on personal taste, but these combinations are worth trying. As a general guideline, try pairing teas with foods from the same geographic region. For example, Japanese green teas taste wonderful with many of the foods indigenous to that country. Here are some other ideas:

Japanese green teas such as sencha, bancha, and genmaicha with seafood, fish, and rice, or to balance out foods high in sodium

Oolong tea with shellfish such as lobster and shrimp

Black teas or a smoky tea such as Lapsang souchong with meat dishes

Pu-erh with meats and poultry

China black teas such as Keemun or Yunnan, or Taiwan oolongs, or Lapsang souchong with hot, spicy foods

Jasmine tea with delicately flavored cooking

BEST TIMES OF DAY
FOR SIPPING VARIOUS TEAS

Breakfast. Try any of the "breakfast" blends, including Irish breakfast and English breakfast, or black teas from Sri Lanka, India (especially from Assam or the second harvest of Darjeeling), or the Yunnan region of China. Prince of Wales and Earl Grey are also good for an early start.

Midmorning and lunch. Green teas, particularly sencha or gunpowder, are appropriate. These are actually great to sip up until midafternoon. Green tea aids digestion and is beneficial when taken with food.

Afternoon. For an afternoon tea, serve an early-harvest Darjeeling or a black tea from China, such as Keemun. For a special occasion, you might serve a special white tea such as Silver Needles or White Peony.

In the late afternoon, try an oolong from Taiwan such as tung ting jade or Iron Goddess of Mercy. Oolongs have less caffeine than black teas. Rooibos, actually a tisane rather than a true tea, makes a sweet addition to an afternoon tea. It is completely free of caffeine but does contain

Caffeine in Tea

The amount of caffeine found in any one cup of tea depends on brewing time, the amount of tea used, and whether the tea is loose or in tea bags, so it's difficult to put a specific number on it. In general, however, black tea contains less than half as much caffeine as coffee. A six-ounce cup of black tea contains about 40 milligrams of caffeine, while a comparable amount of coffee contains between 100 and 120 milligrams. The same amount of green tea contains about 30 milligrams. In general, green and white teas contain the least amount of caffeine, then oolong.

Decaffeinated teas still contain some traces of caffeine. There are two different methods of decaffeinating: using ethyl acetate, which is an organic solvent, and using water and effervescence (carbon dioxide). Both remove caffeine, but only the latter process retains the beneficial polyphenols in the tea. It pays, then, to read labels and determine just how a particular product has been decaffeinated, before purchasing. Herbal teas made from plants other than *Camellia sinensis* usually contain no caffeine, although yerba maté, made from *Ilex paraguariensis*, is quite high in caffeine (or mateine).

antioxidants, making it a great choice for any time of day and a good tisane to give to children.

Evening. Because most teas contain caffeine, don't drink them late in the day or evening, if you are sensitive to the effects of caffeine.

HOW TO BREW
A PERFECT CUP OF TEA

There is not a single rule of brewing tea that applies to all teas, because each tea is unique and deserves individual treatment. There are as many different methods of preparing tea as there are teas. Brewing time varies according to tea type and also personal preference. Experiment and choose the method and the tea that suit you best. The following are suggestions for making the most of your tea:

TEA BAG OR LOOSE TEA?

The first question is whether to use a tea bag or loose tea. In general—and of course there are exceptions—tea in bags is not of as good a quality as loose tea, although the tea industry is changing this rapidly. Many of the better tea companies are combining the quality of loose tea with the ease and convenience of a tea bag—with great success.

An article appearing in a September 2006 *New York Times* reported that many of the largest tea companies, including Lipton, are selling long-leaf (high-quality) teas in bags. They're not using any old bags, however; they're putting this high-quality tea in nylon mesh bags shaped like small pyramids. Many of the smaller companies are following suit, realizing that tea sophistication is growing in the United States, and people are willing to pay for better-quality teas, but that Americans still want the ease and speed of a tea bag.

In the past, the size of the bag limited the size of the leaves that could be put in it. Often fannings, dust, and tea produced by the CTC method (see page 19) are used for tea bags and instant powdered tea, and these are of inferior quality. That is not to say that there are no wonderful tea bags full of the highest-quality teas, but you'll have to look for them, and they will definitely be more expensive than regular tea bags.

WATER

Natural spring water is reputed to be the best for brewing tea, but filtered water does a fine job as well. If you have municipal tap water that tastes of chemicals, definitely filter it before you brew your tea.

Heat the water to boiling for all teas. Take note, though, that for some teas, you'll allow it to cool slightly before you brew it. Warm the teapot (or an individual cup) with a small amount of hot water. Toss out this warming water and then add the tea leaves to the warmed pot or cup. For most teas, use one teaspoon of leaf per cup (eight ounces) of water. After the water comes to a boil, pour it over the tea (with exceptions below).

STEEPING TIME

Use the information below as guidelines for steeping time, but remember that health experts say you need to allow green and black tea to brew at least three to five minutes to obtain the greatest number of antioxidants.

Green tea. For the best taste, allow the boiling water to "rest" for one minute before using. Pour it over the tea and allow it to brew for only one minute. If you're more interested in the maximum health benefits than in the best taste possible, use boiling water and allow the tea to brew for three to five minutes.

White tea. Add eight ounces of water that has been brought to a boil and allowed to cool for one minute. Brew for seven to ten minutes.

Black tea. For whole-leaf tea, brew for five minutes; for broken-leaf, three minutes. For dust, fannings, or CTC (inexpensive tea bags), brew only one or two minutes—these tiny particles of tea brew really quickly. Flavored black teas take five minutes to brew.

Oolong. Brew for five to seven minutes.

Rooibos. Brew for five minutes.

COOKING WITH TEA:
THE POSSIBILITIES

You can also *eat* tea, using it in everything from stir-fry to muffins. This is really not such a far-out idea, since people were eating tea a couple of thousand years ago. It's relatively simple to substitute concentrated tea for liquids in many baking recipes. Sweet breads and muffins seem particularly suited to this substitution.

Diana Rosen, coauthor of *Cooking with Tea*, suggests that if you slowly brew tea at room temperature for about twenty to thirty minutes, the resulting infusion will be free of bitterness and astringency and will be even better than quickly brewed tea in various recipes. Of course, you wouldn't want to drink tea brewed like this, as it would be much too strong. She also suggests using spring water instead of distilled water for a superior product.

Brewed tea can also be used in marinades and basting sauces, or as flavoring for stir-fry. Just be sure to choose a flavor of tea that will enhance your meat or poultry.

Next time you are boiling eggs and want to add something a little unusual, boil the eggs in dark tea, and during the last few minutes of cooking, remove the eggs, crack the shells, and return them to the liquid to continue to cook. This results in a beautiful "marbled" look.

TEA AND HEALTH

TEA HEALTH FACTS

Drinking at least four cups of tea daily offers beneficial results (see below) and may help prevent any number of diseases.

All tea contains cancer-fighting antioxidants, but high-quality green and white teas have them in greater concentrations.

Tea decaffeinated by a water and carbon dioxide process retains 95 percent of its beneficial flavonoids.

Tea must be steeped for at least three to five minutes in hot water to release the greatest concentration of antioxidants.

Tea blends, in which tea is mixed with various substances that do not have antioxidants, have lower concentrations of antioxidants than "pure" teas (for example, a blend that was half tea and half hibiscus flowers would only contain half the antioxidants offered by the same amount of pure tea).

DISEASE-FIGHTING PROPERTIES

Since ancient times in China, people have enjoyed the medicinal benefits of tea. It is not surprising, then, that today many people are turning to tea not only as a tasty and relaxing beverage but also as an aid to fighting many serious diseases. The results are promising, and there is little doubt that drinking tea provides many benefits, though many questions remain unanswered.

Research conducted by highly respected universities and institutes throughout the world has tested the effect of tea consumption on many different ailments and diseases, including cancer (particularly colon, stomach, pancreatic, bladder, esophageal, and breast cancer), rheumatoid arthritis, high cholesterol levels (tea is thought to increase the good HDL cholesterol and lower the bad LDL cholesterol), obesity, osteoporosis, cardiovascular disease, stroke, infection, tooth decay, Alzheimer's disease, the effects of smoking, and impairment of the immune system.

Results have varied widely, and the FDA has refrained from endorsing the health benefits of drinking tea. But, study after study suggested that, without significant side effects, tea (particularly green tea) offers positive results.

Despite indications that drinking tea offers health benefits, it is also clear that it is not a panacea and should not be used as a substitute for fruits, vegetables, and other elements of a healthy diet. Instead, it should be used as a substitute for other beverages, such as coffee and sodas. The *Wellness Letter*, a University of California at Berkeley newsletter, said in a March 2000 article, "Think of it [green tea] as a back-up to a healthy diet and an adjunct to regular exercise and other good health habits—not as a miraculous potion that will keep you well by itself."

Perhaps the greatest benefits of drinking tea are lifestyle choices, rather than the actual chemical composition of the beverage. The simple act of brewing up a cup of tea and stopping long enough to enjoy it probably offers as much benefit as polyphenols or antioxidants or any other element found in the tea plant.

USEFUL WEB SITES

University of Maryland
www.umm.edu/altmed/ConsHerbs/GreenTeach.html

The Pu-erh Web Site
http://pu-erh.net

The Silk Road Foundation
www.silkroadfoundation.org/index.html

The Kenya Tea Development Agency
www.ktdateas.com

The UK Tea Council
www.tea.co.uk

Tea Council of the U.S.
www.teausa.com

Stephen and Martine Batchelor, The Korean Way of Tea
www.stephenbatchelor.org/koreantea.html

Fifteenth-Century Chinese Armada
www.1421.tv

Teahealth
www.teahealth.co.uk

Japan Tea
www.japantea.com

There are countless Web sites posted by various tea companies, many of which offer a lot of information worth exploring.

SELECTED BIBLIOGRAPHY

Blofield, John. *The Chinese Art of Tea*. Boston: Shambhala, 1985.

Buckrell Pos, Tania M. *Tea and Taste: The Visual Language of Tea*. Atglen, Pennsylvania: Schiffer Publishing, 2004.

Bushell, Stephen. *Oriental Ceramic Art*. New York: Crown Publishers, 1980.

Chow, Kit. *All the Tea in China*. San Francisco: China Books and Periodicals Inc., 1990.

Cleary, Thomas, trans. *The Code of the Samurai: A Modern Translation of the Bushido Shoshinshu of Taira Shigesuke*. North Clarendon, Vermont: Tuttle Publishing, 1999.

Fairbanks, John. *China: A New History*. Cambridge, Massachusetts: Belknap Press, 1998.

Fay, Stephen. "China beat Columbus to it, perhaps." *The Economist*, January 4–20, 2006, 80–81.

Feige, Chris and Jeffrey A. Miron. "The Opium Wars, Opium Legalization, and Opium Consumption in China." Discussion Paper Number 2072, Harvard Institute of Economic Research. Cambridge, Massachusetts: Harvard University, May 2005.

Fuquan, Yang. "The 'Ancient Tea and Horse Caravan Road,' the 'Silk Road' of Southwest China." *The Silk Road* 2, no. 1 (2004). Saratoga, California: Silkroad Foundation. Available online at: www.silkroadfoundation.org /newsletter/2004vol2num1/tea.htm.

Gardella, Robert. *Harvesting Mountains: Fujian and the China Tea Trade, 1757–1937.* Berkeley: University of California Press, 1994.

Goodwin, Jason. *The Gunpowder Gardens: Travels through India and China in Search of Tea.* London: Penguin Paperback, 2003.

Hobhouse, Henry. *Seeds of Change: Six Plants That Transformed Mankind.* London: MacMillan, 1992.

Hylton, William H., ed. *The Rodale Herb Book.* Emmaus, Pennsylvania: Rodale Press, 1976.

Lu Yu. *The Classic of Tea.* Translated by Francis Ross Carpenter. Boston: Little, Brown and Co., 1974.

MacFarlane, Iris and Alan MacFarlane. *The Empire of Tea: The Remarkable History of the Plant That Took Over the World.* Woodstock, New York: The Overlook Press, 2003.

MacGregor, David R. *Tea Clippers: Their History and Development, 1833–1873.* London: Percival Marshall and Co., 1952.

Maloney, Justin. "Land Tenure History and Issues in the Republic of Korea." Material prepared for the course Cadastral and Land Information Systems, Department of Spatial Information Science and Engineering, University of Maine, May 2000. Available online at www.spatial.maine.edu/~onsrud/emergingeconomies/country_reports/korea.pdf.

Menzies, Gavin. *1421: The Year China Discovered America*. London: Bantam Press, 2004.

Mintz, Sidney W. *Sweetness and Power: The Place of Sugar in Modern History*. Harmondsworth: Penguin Books Reprint, 1985.

Moxham, Roy. *Tea, Addiction, Exploitation, and Empire*. New York: Carroll and Graf Publishers, 2003.

Okakura, Kakuzo. *The Book of Tea*. North Clarendon, Vermont: Tuttle Publishing, 1989.

Pettigrew, Jane, *The Social History of Tea*. London: The National Trust, 2002.

———. *The Tea Companion*. London: MacMillan Publishers, 1997.

Plutschow, Herbert. "An Anthropological Perspective on the Japanese Tea Ceremony." *Anthropoetics* 5, no. 1 (Spring/Summer 1999). Available online at: www.humnet.ucla.edu/humnet/anthropoetics/apo501/tea.htm.

Podreka, Tomislav. *Serendipitea: A Guide to the Varieties, Origins, and Rituals of Tea.* New York: William Morrow and Company, Inc., 1998.

Prakash, Om. *The Dutch East India Company and the Economy of Bengal, 1630–1720.* Princeton, New Jersey: Princeton University Press, 1985.

Reader's Digest, ed. *Magic and Medicine of Plants.* Pleasantville, New York: Reader's Digest Association, Inc., 1986.

Scott, J.M. *The Great Tea Venture.* New York: E.P. Dutton and Co., 1964.

Sen Soshitsu. *Chado: The Japanese Way of Tea.* New York, Tokyo, Kyoto: Weatherhill/Tankosha, 1979.

Souyri, Pierre François. *The World Turned Upside Down: Medieval Japanese Society.* Translated by Käthe Ross. New York: Columbia University Press, 2001.

Stella, Alain. *The Little Book of Tea.* Paris: Flammarion Editions, 1996.

Suzuki, Daisetz T. *Zen and Japanese Culture.* Princeton, New Jersey: Princeton University Press, reissue, Bollingen Series no. 64, 1970.

Tanaka, Sen'o. *The Tea Ceremony.* New York: Kodansha International Ltd., 1973.

Thomas, Gertrude Z. *Richer Than Spices: How a Royal Bride's Dowry Introduced Cane, Lacquer, Cottons, Tea, and Porcelain to England and So Revolutionized Taste, Manners, Craftsmanship, and History in Both England and America.* New York: Alfred A. Knopf, 1965.

Ukers, William. *All About Tea.* Whitestone, New York: Tea and Coffee Trade Journal Co., 1935.

Whitaker, Jan. *Tea at the Blue Lantern Inn.* New York: St. Martin's Press, 2002.